THE
TRUE
CRIME
PUZZLE BOOK

Dr. Gareth Moore, BSc (Hons) MPhil PhD, is the internationally best-selling author of a wide range of brain-training and puzzle books for both children and adults, including *Enigma: Crack the Code, Ultimate Dot to Dot, Brain Games for Clever Kids, Lateral Logic,* and *Extreme Mazes.* His books have sold millions of copies in the UK alone and have been published in over thirty different languages. He is also the creator of online brain-training site BrainedUp.com and runs the daily puzzle site PuzzleMix.com.

Find him online at DrGarethMoore.com and on Twitter at @DrGarethMoore.

THE TRUE CRIME PUZZLE BOOK

OVER 90 PUZZLING CASES to SOLVE

GARETH MOORE

Published by Sourcebooks
P.O. Box 4410, Naperville, Illinois 60567-4410
(630) 961-3900
sourcebooks.com

Originally published as *The Perfect Crime Puzzle Book* in 2021
in Great Britain by Michael O'Mara Books Limited.

Printed and bound in the United States of America.
VP 10 9 8 7 6 5 4 3 2 1

Introduction

Welcome to *The True Crime Puzzle Book*, where you get to solve puzzles as either the criminal *or* the investigator.

Every puzzle has one of these two icons at the top of its first page:

If you see the magnifying glass, then for this puzzle, you're an investigator. But if you see the CCTV camera, you're a criminal who's trying to get away with some nefarious deed.

Many of the puzzles are a single page or pair of facing pages, but there are also several that take up a bit more space. If you turn to a page in the book, and it doesn't start with a puzzle number and name, just flick backwards a page or two to find the start of the puzzle.

Each puzzle will finish by making clear what it is that you're trying to work out from the information provided, but sometimes the answer you require has been written in one of a number of types of code—so in these cases, you'll often need to look out for hints to help you crack what's going on. These sometimes come in the form of notes that have been found. Other times they are included in the main text or even the title. If you're stuck, try thinking unusually literally about what you're being asked to do.

In a small number of puzzles you'll also need to refer to an existing real-world code to make sense of some information—and for these puzzles you'll find that all of the codes you'll need are included in the "Codes" sections (p. 216) right at the very end of the book, immediately after the Solutions. In fact, you might want to start by taking a look right now, to familiarize yourself with the codes that might pop up elsewhere in the book.

The puzzles are not arranged in any particular order of difficulty, so feel free to dip in and out as you please. With the exception of puzzles 26 to 29, there's also no continuation of story between them, and so it doesn't matter if you start at the end or at the beginning. Or in between. So I suggest you just flick through until something catches your eye and begin there.

I should probably also add that all of the situations in the book are entirely fictional, and any similarity to any existing or historical person or event is entirely coincidental. There may be bad people in the real world, but the ones in this book are entirely pretend and are intended just for fun.

Full solutions are provided at the back of the book, and for any of the puzzles where you must crack a secret code, then a full explanation is generally provided alongside the answer—so if you get stuck, then you could try asking someone nearby to read the solution and give you a hint. Or take a quick peek yourself if there's no one handy! It's better than being stuck forever.

Most importantly of all, remember that the point is to have fun—so if you aren't enjoying a puzzle, then just skip to another one instead. There are almost a hundred of them, so it should take you a while to get through them all!

Good luck!

Dr. Gareth Moore

1. Fast Frequency

The timing's perfect, and you have just fifteen minutes to pull off the heist that you've been planning for over six months.

Your task is to spy on the police by listening in on their radios, but at the last minute, they've changed the frequency they're broadcasting on, and you're running out of time to find it.

You have an analysis tool that scans the airwaves, and it checks six different core frequencies:

3   7   8   9   10   12

It then outputs the list below, showing possible combinations of these frequencies that the police might be broadcasting on. Each combination is a sum of two or more of the core frequencies.

However, you know that the correct frequency will be one that can only be formed by just **one** combination of two or more of the six core frequencies. So, for example, 21 could not be the correct frequency, because it could be formed by both 3 + 8 + 10 and 9 + 12.

Which of these is the correct frequency?

18   22   26   30   34

2. The Phone PIN

You need urgent access to an impounded phone, to discover who your suspect has been talking to before their criminal friends have time to get away.

This particular phone needs exactly four digits to access it. It would take you a long time to try all ten thousand combinations, but luckily you found some notes around the suspect's house that will help. What is their PIN?

Digits increase from left to right

Neighboring digits never have an even difference

The digits add up to 22

There is no zero

The PIN is the highest number that fits these rules

3. Liar, Liar?

One of your colleagues has been undercover in a gang specializing in identity theft. Thanks to her, you have managed to apprehend two gang members, Holly and Harriet.

Your colleague, who you can safely assume is telling you the truth, informed you that in this particular gang, every sentence that each member utters is *always* true or *always* false.

Unfortunately, your colleague was captured by another gang member before she could tell you whether Holly and Harriet were both truth tellers, both liars, or one of each. While other officers go to rescue your captured colleague, can you use these notes gathered from earlier interrogations to work this out?

Holly was very unhappy about being detained and said she has nothing to do with the charges she's been brought in on. Insists she is telling the truth, but that Harriet is a liar.

Harriet strongly denied involvement in any identify theft. Says she is always entirely honest and that neither she nor Holly ever lie.

4. Make Like an Artist

You have passed the initial tests to become part of a criminal gang, and the boss is starting to trust you, so he tells you that they have been planning a major art heist for the last few months. You're on the team to help. Right at this very moment, the forger

is working on his pièce de résistance—a copy of Gaumonet's famous *Twintersection*, which they plan to replace the original with after they steal it from the gallery.

Can you help him to make it an even more exact replica by spotting his ten mistakes on the reproduction on the page below? And for an added challenge, see if you can find them all within five minutes.

5. The Apartment Crime

A terrible murder has been committed, and it's down to the force's finest to work out what happened. Unfortunately they are all on a team retreat, so perhaps you can help instead?

You've narrowed down the area the murderer came from to a particularly notorious apartment block on Steel Street, where each of the apartments is numbered from 1 to 1,000.

The victim was popular in the community, so an unusually large number of tip-offs have come your way. Here's what they say:

- Dave tells you:
  "The apartment number is one that reads exactly the same even if you stand on your head and look at it."

- Sam informs you:
  "I know for a fact that the first digit of the apartment number is greater than the last digit of the apartment number."

- Monica reveals that:
  "The sum of the digits in the apartment number is equal to a square number."

What apartment number does the murderer live in?

6. The Sign on the Safe

You're on a big job, and you've made it all the way to the victim's hidden safe. Congratulations! But there's just one problem—it's refusing to fall to your usual safe cracking techniques.

You're about to give up, when all of a sudden your luck changes, and you find what could prove to be a very useful sign. Could this provide the necessary set of eight digits?

What two digits will complete the nonmathematical sequence—and then hopefully unlock the safe?

Don't forget the unlock code for the safe!

4 6 3 6 4 3 ? ?

7. Caught by Clothing

There's a manhunt on for an infamous thief, and you're in charge of managing the hotline.

You've had a number of tip-offs that he was hiding out at a local hotel, so officers have gone to the scene to see what evidence they can collect.

By the time they get there, he's already checked out, and his room has been cleaned—but he seems to have accidentally left some of his clothing behind, and it's been put in a lost-property bag.

Unfortunately the hotel does not know which bag it was, since there were a few other forgetful guests who were all on site, each claiming one of five lost property bags, when officers arrived.

Can you use the other guests' statements to work out which lost property bag is whose? The remaining bag must contain the thief's clothing, which can then be taken away for DNA testing.

- **Guest 1**: I definitely lost my belt.

- **Guest 2:** I left behind my favorite watch.

- **Guest 3:** I can't believe I forgot to put on my tie!

- **Guest 4:** I somehow managed to leave without my socks.

Bag A

Belt
Watch

Bag B

Gloves
Scarf
Belt

Bag C

Tie
Belt
Gloves

Bag D

Scarf
Socks
Tie
Watch

Bag E

Scarf
Gloves

8. All Mapped Out

A rival criminal is encroaching on your turf, and you want to find where he's based and make it clear to him who's boss around here.

Based on intercepted phone data from a friend up high, you've narrowed down his secret base to somewhere in the map area shown opposite.

Just today you've received some cryptic tip-offs, perhaps from a member of his gang who is looking to curry favor with you.

Can you identify the precise location, based on the following tip-off clues?

- When I first visited their hideaway, they picked me up from a bridge over some train tracks.
- We drove until we reached a roundabout, but we didn't cross any other roads on the way. We drove straight over the roundabout.
- Next, we got to a fork in the road and took the road that went off to the right. The driver kept going until we reached a second roundabout, and he took the first exit.
- When we reached the first junction we came to, we turned to the right and then got into another car. The car then drove to the very next junction, then turned right again.
- We got out of the car at the end of that road and went into an abandoned building on the right.

Can you draw an "X" on the map to indicate the location of the rival's hideout?

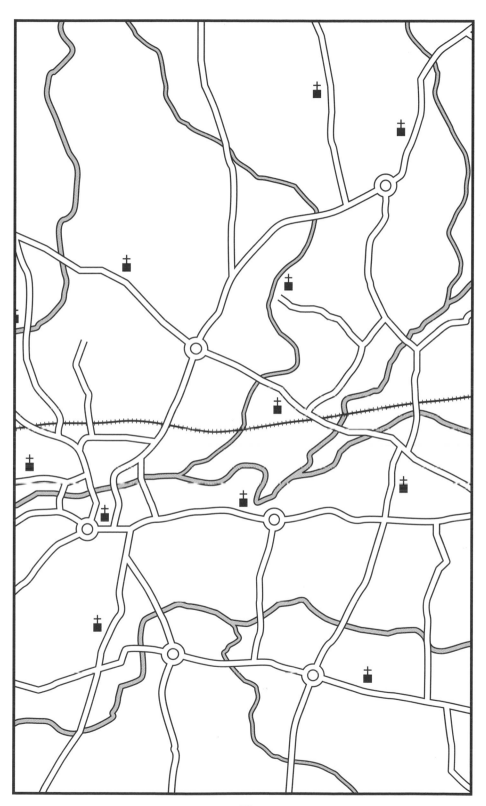

9. The Missing Diplomat

Diplomatic duties can throw those committed souls, whose life's work is to obey strange orders without question, into some unusual and challenging circumstances.

Tiptoeing along the tightropes of intergovernmental relationships never appealed much to me as a career path—the life of a detective inspector is much easier to my mind. However, the twilight world of the diplomat overlapped with mine when I was put in charge of investigating the mysterious disappearance of Mr. Basil Hatton, a civil servant in Her Majesty's service.

Mr. Hatton had, it seemed, been sent away on a work trip to Madrid (although I was unable to verify that it *was* a work trip), whereupon he vanished off the face of the earth. It was upon my shoulders to find the missing man and to ascertain if any of the circumstances surrounding his disappearance were at all suspicious. In fact, I was tempted to catch a plane to Madrid at my first convenience to try to get to the bottom of the affair. But somehow, my instinct stopped me, and I resolved to conduct some interviews in the UK first to paint a picture of the missing man.

I began my inquiries by speaking to Basil's line manager, a jovial gentleman of some fifty-odd years. I asked him to give me a brief account of Basil Hatton's personality and work life:

"I can't say that he was a spectacularly memorable civil servant—but I suppose that made him suited to carrying out those tasks that required some discretion. He'd been based in these offices in London for some years now and seemed quite content in his routine. He never talked much about his personal life, but I know that he liked to walk to and from work each day. He rented a place from his sister-in-law not too far away—seemed to spend the evenings cooking and reading for the most part. I wouldn't say he was either particularly sociable or reclusive, but everyone on the team got along with him well. One thing did strike me as odd recently though—a letter came through for him that seemed to shake him up a bit, looked as if it might have been from the Foreign Office. After he'd read it, he said that he had to leave for Madrid as soon as possible—didn't look too happy about it either."

After my call, I decided to pay a visit to Mr. Hatton's landlady. It appeared that, in addition to owning Basil's apartment, she was a resident in it too, in a locked room set off to the side of the hallway. She was not the most effusive of interviewees, and despite her regular proximity to the missing man, I learned nothing more than that he had left as usual for work on Tuesday morning but had not returned in the evening. I therefore left the house without much more information than I had entered with, and returned home to my wife for dinner.

At Basil's office the next day, I managed to track down a couple of members of his team who were willing to speak with me. A researcher who occupied the desk next to the missing man's was most helpful:

"He has always been a loyal chap and keen to help—it must be quite a situation in Spain therefore. Of course, he's fluent in Spanish, so I suppose it adds up—comes in quite useful for international conferences and such like. But it was a sudden departure, I'll give you that. He mentioned that he'd received a letter on Monday—he packed up his things on Tuesday, and by Wednesday he was gone completely. I wondered if there might be something personal going on that he wasn't telling us—he's a nice man, but he can be quite reserved; one never quite knows what he's thinking. That probably comes of being an only child."

One of his other colleagues chipped in at this point:

"I did hear him speaking with one of his Spanish contacts
last week—it sounded somewhat heated, but they seemed to be
laughing by the end of it. I'll try to get the phone number for you if you
like—his assistant will have it, but she's out at the moment."

I let them know that I would be grateful to receive any further
information they had to offer and took my leave.

My next port of call was the Foreign Office—it was not far from Basil's
offices, and I decided to drop in on the off chance that I would be
able to speak to someone. I had not expected to have any luck, but
was somewhat shocked and pleasantly surprised when I was quickly
ushered into a small office to speak to a government aide who claimed
responsibility for Basil's letter.

"Yes, Basil is exactly the kind of person we need in Madrid for this
case,' he said, speaking in the deliberate, clipped tones that government
work seems to instill in people. "Someone with his level of experience
and a polite manner, unassuming, never married (you know how
family can make things difficult in this line of work)—and did you
know he's fluent in Spanish? Quite an asset to us in this situation; the
people we're dealing with don't take kindly to English foreigners who
don't make an effort. Of course we couldn't tell his colleagues why he
had to go. All far above their security clearance. But I know Basil—we
met when we were both starting out our careers in the Cabinet Office;
we've been friends ever since. I know I can trust him."

I left the building and began to amble slowly along the Thames Path,
watching the mudlarkers combing the shore below. As I walked, I felt
my phone buzzing, and when I answered, I was greeted by a woman
who introduced herself as Basil's assistant. I was pleased to hear from
her, having missed her earlier in the day. It seemed that Basil had
phoned her on Tuesday afternoon to inform her that he was leaving the
country for a while. He had been brief and businesslike, giving her no

reason to suspect that anything was amiss, but her suspicions had been raised by an email that she had received the following day. It was from an acquaintance of Basil's, someone in need of financial assistance, who wanted to meet with him. She had forwarded it to him, but had received no response.

I considered all of the information I had gathered, and it seemed that Mr. Hatton might have landed himself in a sticky situation. I felt sure there was one person in particular who had said something that didn't quite make sense. But who had been lying to me—and what was the lie? I needed to review my notes to work it out.

Can you find the contradiction in the stories? Who do you think was lying?

10. The Artful Dodger

It takes a specialist to steal something from a heavily protected museum, but that's exactly what you are. You never managed to win an Olympic gold for your gymnastic skills—or, frankly, get anywhere near winning one—but they've certainly come in handy since you started your lucrative career in evading security systems.

After some extensive surveillance work, the floor plan of a major art museum, opposite, has been augmented to show the areas covered by all twenty of its security cameras.

Night has now fallen, and the museum is closed, and you've just managed to gain entrance to the front of the building via a spare key that a crooked caretaker slipped you earlier in the day.

How do you make your way from the entrance all the way through to the trove of ancient coins, marked with a picture of a coin, without being seen by any security cameras?

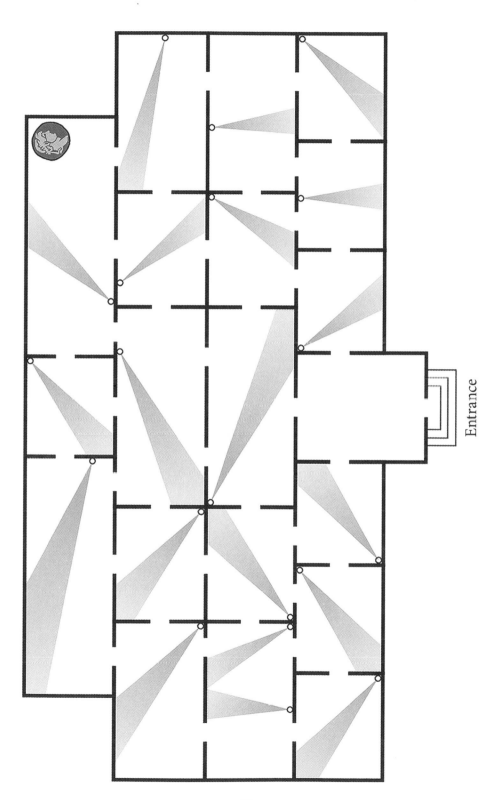

Entrance

11. The Four Robbers

A private bank vault has been targeted by a band of robbers. You have managed to apprehend the four criminals responsible, but not before they hid the gold bars they stole—and, unfortunately, the owner of the vault can't remember how many were in it.

Fortunately for you, the suspects that you've apprehended are more than willing to discuss how many gold bars they each took—although they don't seem to realize they're incriminating themselves while they accuse their friends of greed.

The following statements were taken from each of the criminals:

Criminal A: We had agreed that we would each collect different quantities of gold bars, as we all had different jobs to do. Each of us who arrived at the vault was to take half of the gold bars there, plus an extra two. I was in charge of hacking the vault security system—the most difficult job—and was the first one to get into the vault. As agreed, I took half of all of the gold bars there, plus two extra.

Criminal B: I was the second one to get into the vault—I had been making sure our getaway car was ready. I didn't think it was a very fair system, but yes, I took half of the bars that were left in the vault, and an extra two on top of that.

Criminal C: I was in charge of stopping the security guards coming in. I eventually managed to lock them into a different vault, but it took a while, so I was the third one to get to the vault with the gold bars. I filled up my bag with half of what was there, and then put two extra bars in my pockets.

Criminal D: I was the last one to go in. I had been disabling all of the computers and telephones in the building to buy us some time. I was furious when I got to the vault—the rest of those swindling delinquents had taken all of the gold already and there was absolutely none left! So I'm innocent, really, don't you think?

You're not inclined to agree—they all seem pretty guilty to you. But your job is just to work out how many gold bars there were in the vault to start with, before they took them all.

How many were there?

12. Blinded by the Light

Your boss in a smuggling ring has told you to look out for a coded message telling you the name of a contact you'll meet at the next drop, and instructed you to keep an eye on the abandoned tower block near the harbor.

This evening, some of the windows have mysteriously lit up; you suspect it could be the message you've been waiting for, but it's not Morse code—could it be braille?

Crack the code to find out who you'll be meeting when the time comes.

13. Digital Disguise

A member of your crime syndicate is in prison—but this doesn't stop them from contributing to your activities. While inside, they have learned the access code for the HQ of a rival crime organization—if you can get inside the building where they base themselves, you might be able to learn all kinds of information.

Naturally, your source had to disguise the code, and all they have given you is this series of sketches and a short message.

PM   AM   PM

You're looking for a twelve-digit number.
You have twenty-four hours a day
to work it out!

14. Find the Apartment

You have received a tip-off from a gang member who has become frustrated with his boss and wants him out of the picture. He has sent you a note with the boss's apartment number. Fantastic! You know which apartment complex this wanted criminal lives in, but this is the final piece of the puzzle.

To make sure he didn't get caught, your informant has encoded the information. Can you work out what the note says and deduce the gang leader's apartment number? The first digit is given, but what are the second and third digits?

Note: Use <u>segmented</u> thinking

$$4 + 3 = 9$$

$$5 + 2 = ?$$

$$1 + 5 = ?$$

15. The Eccentric Enigma

You have been instructed to pick up a valuable delivery of stolen jewels from the house of an eccentric but brilliant criminal mastermind. However, when you arrive at the arranged time, she is not there, and you have no idea where the jewels are hidden.

The house is a mess, with scraps of paper, musical instruments, scientific equipment, and books scattered everywhere. You eventually find a safe under a desk with a numbered keypad on it. On the desk is a note with your name on it, weighted down with a compass:

N—S

NW—NE—E—W—SW—SE

NE—NW—W—E—SE—SW

NW—NE—S

Find the code, and you will find the jewels!

Remember to only travel using straight lines.

Can you crack the code and gain entry to the safe?

16. Home Sweet Home

One of your sharper detective sergeants has been working on tracking down a gang you've been hunting for a while but never seem able to find any evidence against.

Recently, you've been trying to find physical addresses for the members; they're all active online, but you think your best chance of obtaining evidence is to conduct a proper search in their homes.

He's looking into a potential connection between the way the members of the gang encode their names on social media and their addresses.

Based on his notes, it looks like he's on the cusp of a breakthrough.

This detective sergeant has only just left the office when you get an urgent call—you've had a tip-off that the whole gang is about to meet in a shopping mall for a robbery.

You see a chance to send some staff to search the houses of the criminals concerned while you head out to face the gang. But you have to work out what your sergeant's notes mean first…

All you need to work out is their house numbers—and then you'll have everything you need to take them down. It looks like he's already worked out two of them. What are the other three?

Criminal – Real Name	Criminal – Online Name	Address – Road Name	Address – Number
Marcus Leary	Bpgrjh Atpgn	Hannover Place	15
Cathy Jaydon	Jhaof Qhfkvu	Green Lane	7
Jesse Winton	Xsggs Kwbhcb	Fairchild Avenue	?
Larry Orsino	Mbssz Pstjop	High Street	?
Helga Smith	Spwrl Dxfes	Dark Hill	?

How are the suspects creating their online names—and where does each of them live?

17. Mugged Off

An eyewitness has given you the following description of a criminal who robbed the corner shop, and is reviewing the mugshots in the rogues gallery opposite. The gallery contains pictures of six petty thieves who are known to work in the same area.

Here's what they said:

- He didn't seem to me to be particularly tall or particularly short, so I'd say he wasn't the tallest person here at any rate.

- He definitely didn't have any piercings—well, not on his head, anyway!

- He might have had a scar on his face. Or perhaps it was a big wrinkle? But it was definitely one of the two. And definitely no freckles.

- Oh yeah, I should have said this to start with! He wasn't completely bald.

- Now I think about it, he definitely had a scar on the left side of his face—left as you look at him, I mean.

- Does that help? That's all I can remember.

Who is the eyewitness describing?

ROGUES GALLERY OF KNOWN THIEVES

18. Gate-Crashing

You have intercepted an email from one criminal to another with the heading, "New gate passcode." This could prove really useful next time you need to "visit" their property!

When you open the email, however, it doesn't contain any numbers at all—just a strange map and a series of directions.
The number must be hidden somehow…

NEW GATE PASSCODE

INSTRUCTIONS - PACKAGE DELIVERIES

Day 1: Pick up a package from Jem's corner shop, then go straight to the boss's apartment to get his signature. From here, take the package straight to the gang HQ.

Day 2: Pick up a package from the garage southwest of the police station - take it to the bank, and meet your partner there. Together, head to the telephone booth southwest of the fire station, and phone your getaway driver. Then, go to the car park to meet them.

Day 3: Pick up a package at the bank (meet your associate in the queue). Take it to the gang HQ, but stop at the hospital on your way - there's something you need to check. Head northeast to the garage from here to collect your car, then go to the nearest telephone booth to call the boss and confirm all has gone to plan.

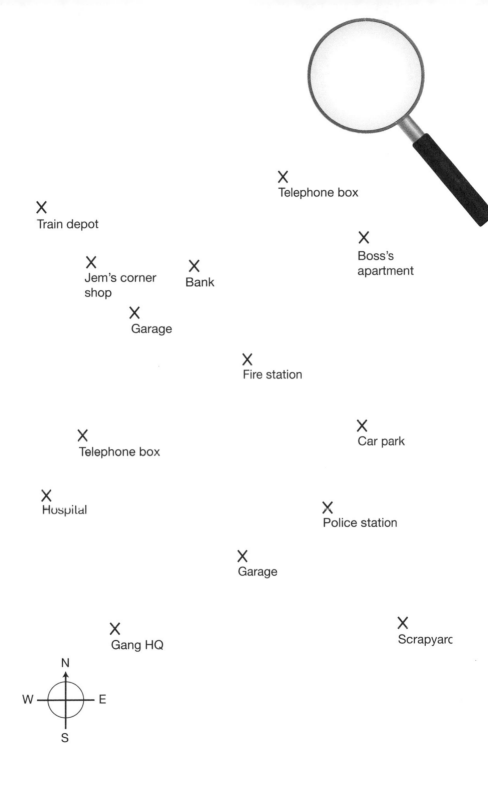

X
Telephone box

X
Train depot

X
Jem's corner
shop

X
Bank

X
Boss's
apartment

X
Garage

X
Fire station

X
Telephone box

X
Car park

X
Hospital

X
Police station

X
Garage

X
Gang HQ

X
Scrapyard

N
W ⊕ E
S

19. Hack the Hacker

An anonymous source has hand-delivered a memory stick to your head office, which contains files stolen from one of the country's top hackers. However, the memory stick is passcode-protected.

A few clues pop up on the screen when you plug in the stick—the passcode seems to use a code where symbols stand in for numbers.

Can you work out the numerical value of each symbol and then use those values to work out the passcode? Each symbol represents a whole number.

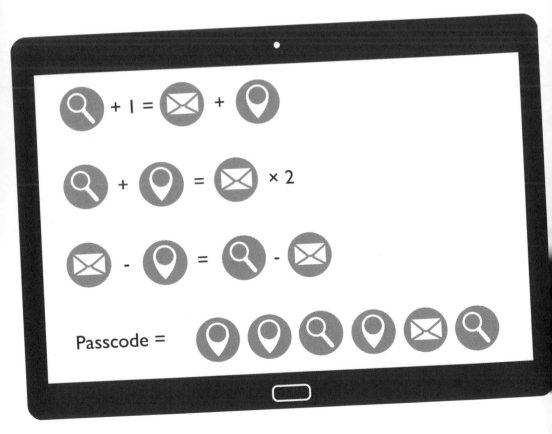

20. Multifaceted Problem

You have pulled off a heist that has put you in possession of a cache of valuable jewels—but you need to offload them, and fast, before the police catch on.

You've been given the name of a jewelry fence—the best in the business—but your contact has encoded the phone number to protect the criminal's identity.

Can you solve the cipher your contact has sketched out to reveal the number?

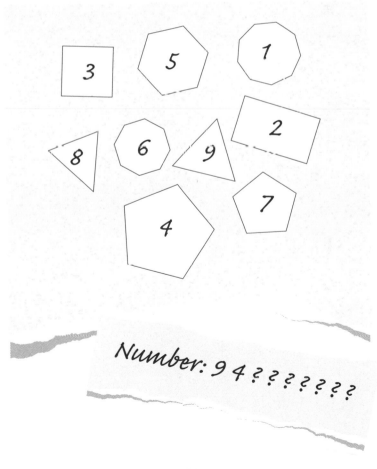

Number: 9 4 ? ? ? ? ? ? ?

21. Villainous Vacation

A serial killer is on the loose! Weirdly, he likes to send warnings in advance—in groups of three at a time.

Shortly before each set of murders, he sends a set of visual clues to the police to reveal where his latest atrocities are planned to take place.

So far the police have failed to get to any of the locations in time, but perhaps you can help.

Work with the CSI team to see if you can identify all of these locations and maximize your chances of catching him before his next kill.

Location 1

- Pictured at the top of this page. Thought to be somewhere in mainland Europe.

Location 2

- Pictured above. Thought to be somewhere in the continental US.

Location 3

- Pictured to the right. Thought to be on a different continent from the previous two pictures. Likely to be a major tourist attraction in its particular country.

22. Old-School Cool

You're part of a notorious gang that rather incongruously speaks to each other in an emoji code.

You're second-in-command for the planning of the next heist, and the powers that be have sent you the following code to let you know the three initials of your next target.

Message 1:

Message 2:

Message 3:

Message 4:

Gotta dash to be there on the dot!

Can you work out from these messages who the next victim is going to be? Or at least, what their initials are?

23. Whispered Words

You've stopped by your local cafe after a long day, and as you sit down with your coffee, you hear snippets of a conversation. A man and a woman are whispering, but it's loud enough to make out the details. They're planning a theft—and guess what? It's happening tomorrow! Here's what you manage to gather from their whispers:

- Target of crime: a high-end jewelry shop situated on Bond Street

- The man and woman are planning to pretend to be looking for wedding rings

- They have booked an appointment at 3 p.m. for a consultation

- They will express interest in gold and diamond rings

- When several rings are laid out for them to inspect, they will hold the jewelers at gunpoint, take the rings, and make their escape

- A Ford Mondeo will be waiting outside to take them to the house of a corrupt banker in Mayfair, who is in on the plan

You don't want to be seen writing any notes, so you don't draw attention to yourself. You know, though, that you'll need to get back to the office and relay as much information to your partner as soon as you can. Spend a couple of minutes memorizing the above information, and then turn the page to see if you can recall the crucial details for your colleague.

Make sure you read the previous page before you answer these questions.

You're back in the office and manage to find your partner to tell him what you've heard. He's got a lot of questions for you; can you answer them?

1.   Which precious stones were the criminals interested in?

2.   What kind of getaway car were they planning to use?

3.   What street is the robbery supposed to take place on?

4.   How many people were planning to conduct the robbery?

5.   What time was the consultation booked?

6.   Where is the corrupt banker located?

24. Missing Mole

You're a top internet hacker who has been commissioned to infiltrate a university's computer system in order to retrieve some documents about a new breakthrough in molecular physics.

All was going to plan until you discovered the documents are password protected. You manage to find a "password reminder" email, which seems to be in some sort of code:

Password reminder:

The key is on the table:

E 53 7 16 52 53 7

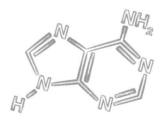

What table could they be referring to—and therefore what is the password?

25. Pick Your Poison

You've been closing in on a mob boss for a long time now, and you think you've gathered enough evidence to bring him to justice.

You get a call from your superior, and you're pretty sure it's time to gear up and get ready for a raid—but he's calling with bad news. The mob boss—who's been in hiding for a few days—has been found dead in his hideout. This isn't what you expected.

You go to his hideout together and try to piece together what's happened. He was wanted by a lot of people, so there are plenty of suspects, but at first it doesn't seem like there's been any foul play.

Your team has been watching the hideout apartment since he started his isolation—since you have spies everywhere—and nobody has been to visit the apartment, except for his girlfriend on the first day, but she left soon afterwards. So how did he die?

You find a list of scrawled diary entries by the boss's bedside—he'd obviously decided that journaling would be the way to get through this period of confinement.

Day 1 – Sophie came round to drop off a lasagna—she knows I'm going into hiding. Sweet girl. Lasagna tasted delicious, same as always. She's a great cook, always reliable.

Day 2 – Not feeling so great today—stomach pain all morning, though managed to eat some

more lasagna for lunch. Plenty
of leftovers to get me through the week.
What would I do without Sophie?

Day 3 — Had terrible nightmares. Woke up but
still seeing strange nightmarish things in my
room. Feeling like I might throw up all morning
so stayed in bed.

Day 4 — Woke up to hair all over my pillow.
Thought it was another hallucination, but no,
it's really my hair. Is it the stress of the hideout?

Day 5 — Tried to make it over to the window
for some fresh air, but think slippers don't fit
anymore—too painful to walk in. Feet feel like
they're on fire. What on earth is going on?

At first there's not that much to help you here, although it seems like
your victim was in a bad way before he died.

You get a call from the autopsy guys, who think that your mob boss has been poisoned with something, though they haven't run all the tests yet. That seems to fit with these diary entries— so you decide to take the diary to the team at the lab to piece together the clues.

When you arrive at the autopsy, you show the team a copy of the diary entries. In return, they show you a list of poisons they've narrowed it down to and how they work.

Strychnine

Strychnine poisoning leads to muscle spasms and convulsions, followed by paralysis of neural pathways that control breathing, leading to asphyxiation. Death occurs within two to three hours of exposure.

Arsenic

Signs of arsenic poisoning include headaches, confusion, drowsiness, severe diarrhea, and vomiting blood, along with stomach pains, muscle cramps, convulsions, and seizures. Hair loss is present in chronic cases. Death by coma is common in severe cases. In acute cases, death occurs within two hours to four days.

Atropine

Atropine toxicity symptoms include warm, dry skin and decreased sweating, blurred vision caused by enlarged pupils, hallucinations, and, in severe cases, coma. It is very difficult to detect in autopsy but has a pronounced bitter taste.

Cyanide

Cyanide poisoning leads to seizures and convulsions, inability to breathe easily, and, in severe cases, coma.

Death is by cardiac arrest and occurs within two to five minutes of ingestion.

Amanita phalloides

Poisoning by death cap mushroom leads to abdominal pain, diarrhea, nausea, and vomiting, jaundice, delirium, seizures and coma. The toxin leads to liver, and kidney failure, and death in occurs six to sixteen days after exposure.

Thallium

Thallium poisoning causes abdominal pain, nausea, and vomiting, as well as nerve damage (the palms and soles of feet become very painful), anxiety, confusion, and hallucinations. Hair loss can occur at low dosages. It is colorless, tasteless, and water soluble.

You're pretty sure that Sophie is a suspect now—but how did she do it? Can you work out from the journal which of these poisons was most likely to have been used to take down the mafia boss?

26. Passcode Problem

You are involved in a big heist along with several associates, one of whom has been working undercover at a hedge fund. You're hoping to infiltrate their security system and, eventually, make off with millions.

The hedge fund team is away on an exclusive business trip—your associate included—so it's the perfect time to break into their head office to case the joint. You want to call your associate to get information, but their calls are being monitored—they can only answer calls from the hedge fund office.

You'll need to break into the office building via the back door, but it's protected with a passcode, which your friend seemingly failed to give you. Before they left, however, they gave you a newspaper, folded to show the puzzle section—and now you notice that there are four sudoku puzzles, some of which have notes beside them.

Your associate is obviously intending for you to solve the puzzles to reveal the codes you'll need while he's away. He's scrawled a note on one of the puzzles, which says:

Office: middle block, middle row, left to right, 3 digits

You decide to start with this puzzle.

		8		7		1		
	9		3		4		5	
2			9		8			4
	2	6				7	4	
1								6
	4	7				5	8	
6			1		3			2
	1		4		9		3	
		9		2		4		

Hopefully this three-digit code will be the passcode you need.
Can you solve the sudoku and then say what it is?

27. Dangerous Dialing

You have successfully broken into the office building! Now what?

It's time to phone your associate for more instructions, but you realize you don't know their work cell phone number. At least you can now call them from the office phone without being blocked.

You have a look back at the puzzle page and can see they've written, "If in doubt, phone a friend," next to another sudoku puzzle. Thinking about it, you realize you know that their phone number must be nine digits long and start with a 5.

Can you solve the puzzle and phone your friend before anyone catches you? Assume the required number reads horizontally.

4								8
			1	6	4			
		9	7		5	3		
	1	8				5	2	
	6			9			1	
	4	2				9	6	
		6	3		7	1		
			8	5	9			
8								9

28. Open the Vault

Nice one. You've deciphered the phone number! You call your associate, and they tell you that a third sudoku conceals the access code for the fund manager's bank account. Once you have this, you'll be able to hack into his online account and move money to anywhere in the world. So much for casing the joint—this heist just heated up! Your associate hangs up, but not before they tell you that a diagonal adding up to 44 has what you need. It's time to solve the third puzzle:

3			9		5			6
		1					9	
	7		3		6		5	
1		3				2		8
				6				
8		7				5		1
	2		6		4		7	
		6				3		
4			1		9			2

When you've completed the puzzle, you find your way to the portal for the company's accounts and see the following. What do you type?

Enter passcode: 4

29. Double-Crossed?

You put the access code into the boss's computer—and to your horror, an alarm blares out above your head. The sound is deafening. An error message flashes up on the screen:

SUSPECTED UNAUTHORIZED ENTRY

ENTER FAIL-SAFE CODE: _ _ _ _

YOU HAVE 1 ATTEMPT LEFT

10 MINUTES UNTIL EMERGENCY SYSTEM SHUTDOWN

DOORS ARE LOCKED

You start to panic—has your associate set you up?

You glance at the phone—but you don't have enough time to call your associate and work out what's happening—especially not if they've led you into a trap. There's a final sudoku that hasn't been completed, but there are no instructions next to it. What should you do?

Suddenly, you get a text on your own phone from an unknown number—then you realize it's your associate's company mobile number, the one you decoded earlier. The message says:

There are traitors everywhere—EVEN AT THE BOTTOM!

You're not sure if you can trust him anymore, but with the alarm still blaring and the risk of being locked inside the building for the police to find you, you decide your friend has given you a final clue. But first you'll need to solve the last sudoku before you can discover the four-digit code.

	3	2				1	4	
7			2		5			6
6								7
	7		1		4		2	
				7				
	5		8		2		3	
1								3
5			9		3			8
	9	7				5	1	

What's the fail-safe code?

30. Taking Names

You are on the hunt for a notorious criminal gang who has been remotely disabling the security systems in major art galleries all over the world so that a team on the ground can sweep in and steal priceless artifacts.

After months of investigation, you think you're finally getting closer to the hackers, and you've found the physical address that they're controlling their operations from.

When you raid their apartment, there's nobody there—but you find a memory stick labeled "Targets' on their desk.

This must be too good to be true—why would they have left it in plain sight?

Sure enough, when you open the file, you find a list of what looks like names and dates, along with a message apparently from the gang with the subject "FAO the Police':

Congratulations - you've found our base. Yay you! Sadly, there's nothing you can do to stop today's takedown, but just for fun here's our timeline for the people we'll be targeting later this year:

Greg Hunter: 01/02

Hedwig Green: 06/01

Violet Marston: 05/07

Anisha Peele: 05/05

Delilah Malik: 04/01

You look closely at the taunting message, hoping you can solve the clue in time to alert the right people.

In fact, you're sure these aren't the names of real targets, and perhaps they are actually hiding the location of today's job. Criminals can be pretty cocky, especially when they think the police will never catch on to their oh-so-clever codes.

Where is today's target?

31. Blooming Heck

A criminal has stolen a rare flower specimen and you're pretty sure he's hidden it in plain sight—right here, in the botanical gardens!

You've narrowed down the likely location to the work area shown opposite. Can you spot the valuable orchid in the middle of all the others?

Luckily you have a photograph that was taken shortly before it was stolen, which should help you successfully locate the precious plant. See how long it takes you to find it, Detective.

32. The Drop

Martin isn't a bad person, exactly. He's a great boss; he's kind to his employees, respects our working hours, and pays us fairly. He's funny, reserved, and enjoys growing vegetables in his spare time. I personally don't have a bad word to say about him.

It's just that he's also the head of an international organized cybercrime ring, and a lot of people tend to disagree with that sort of thing.

I've been working with Martin for years—ten of them, specifically. When I met him he'd already been running his "team'—that's what he called it—for a few years, but he welcomed me in like a family member. I'd met him online, in an encrypted chat room: I'd heard his name being pinged around in some shady circles, and I wanted to find out more about the man behind the myth.

He was always talked about as a kind of Robin Hood figure—he developed and sent out ransomware to rival criminal gangs, freezing their assets and occasionally draining them of their funds if they didn't play fair. He usually had pretty reasonable demands: stop fleecing rich old widows out of their life savings, stop draining major accounts that are supposed to be used for charity work, stop hacking our preferred targets before we can get to them, that sort of thing.

A few months ago, one of our biggest rivals crossed a line. Pretty much everything we do is online, but these guys had managed to find out the location of our physical base: it's a small storage unit with a lot of hardware and some pretty sensitive information. And a few stacks of banknotes. Someone had managed to gain access—and they'd done it using an actual key—and made off with some important data on a memory stick, as well as helping themselves to a few of the banknotes. They sent us a cheerful message to let us know they'd dropped in.

Martin tried all the usual tactics: drained their accounts, sent them a virus worm to destroy their setup, made some very believable threats. They could keep the money if they wanted—it was counterfeit anyway, so they wouldn't get far with that—but that memory stick was coming back to us, or else. The thieves with our data had only one demand: they wanted to speak to Martin in person, see him in the flesh, and then they would hand over the memory stick with our incriminating data on it. That's it. It seemed too good to be true, but Martin went for it. It's refreshing, he said, to meet people in real life after scamming them online for so many years. Perhaps they could talk it out, organize a truce. Anything to get the memory stick back.

It was a trap, of course; we should have been it coming. It was an ambush, but not the kind we planned for: as soon as Martin arrived, he was surrounded by police. Police? *That* was a surprise. Whoever we'd been in contact with was either an undercover police unit, or our rivals had tipped them off. The second option seems pretty unlikely—what criminal gang wants to buddy up with the police?—so it dawned on us that one of our own must have been feeding information to the outside and, what's worse, must have used their own key to take part in the "break-in".

So anyway, Martin's behind bars for a while, and he wants me to find out who the traitor is.

There were five keys to the storage unit, and five people were trusted with them. Martin and I had one each, and there were three others on the team who had a key: Sara, Jacques, and Leon. They'd all come straight over to the storage unit after the break-in and were equally troubled when Martin started his sojourn in jail, so nobody had ostensibly crossed over to the dark side.

Martin was above suspicion and so he claimed, was I. That said, it was my job to find out what they'd all been doing on the day of the break-in, where they kept their keys, and, well, whether one of the three of them had ratted us out to the police.

The break-in was a week ago, on a Thursday. It happened early in the morning—around 5 a.m., according to some security footage—and whoever got in had sent us a message half an hour later saying they had the memory stick and wanted to talk. I started by asking Leon what he'd been doing on Thursday morning—and where he usually kept his keys.

"I was asleep! Fast asleep. You know me, a late riser. Jacques had been over the night before, Wednesday night. We played a few video games; it's nice to hang out with a real person instead of just online, you know, instead of using headsets and usernames. We played a few rounds of a stupid go-kart racing game I'd gotten and then ordered a pizza, and he left around ten p.m. I was so tired I was asleep by eleven p.m., I think—I have some flawless blackout blinds that mean I sleep so solidly, I was dead to the world. The key is taped to the bottom of a drawer on my nightstand. I don't think I've used it since last year, because I never go the storage place alone—I'm always with you or Martin.

"When I heard the place had been broken into I checked the key was still there, and it was—same place; tape hadn't moved—and nobody had been in while I was sleeping 'cause I lock everything from the inside when I close up for the night. I woke up around eight a.m., and I had a message from the boss about the break-in, so I hopped in the shower and joined him at the storage place about an hour after you got there, eight thirty, I think? So I'm not much help to you at all—I was asleep the whole time with my key right next to me. Sara sent me a message in the night about going for a run first thing, so I know she was up in the early morning, but she keeps pretty

strange hours anyway. She's a night owl.
Have you heard from the boss?'

I said I had—but I didn't tell Leon it's because I'd
been told to find out who'd betrayed us from the
inside. Next I found Jacques, and asked him the same thing: where had he
been, and where were his keys?

"Wednesday night I went over to Leon's; we played some dumb
video games and had a pizza, and I walked home around ten p.m.
I'd never been round to his place before, and it's pretty small, a little
ground floor apartment, pretty dark and dank, but that's because he
keeps his blinds closed—says it helps him sleep, or something. I got
home about eleven p.m.—I walked slowly, since his place isn't that
far from mine. I messaged a few gamers I know to see if they were
up for playing, but the whole world seemed to be asleep. I just had a
shower and got into bed around midnight, fell asleep straight away.

"I woke up about two a.m. to a message back from one of the
gamers, and I couldn't get back to sleep, so I played a few games
online with them. Sara messaged at about four fifteen a.m. asking
if I wanted to go on a run—she's a strange girl, always up in the
night—and since I still couldn't sleep, and Sara said there was a
decent sunrise on the way, I put some clothes on and joined her.
We ran past Leon's place, and Sara tried to see if he was awake
and wanted to join, but she couldn't get ahold of him—I guess he
was still asleep—so it was just the two of us. We got back around
six a.m.—everything was so quiet outside—and I made Sara an
omelette round my place.

"She was just about to leave when we got a message from Martin to
meet him at the storage unit, about seven a.m., I think, and we were
there in half an hour—just after you. As for the key, I had it with
me the whole time; it's on the same ring of keys as my apartment,
so it comes with me everywhere—even on the run with Sara at the

crack of dawn. In fact—I've got it here. But I guess we'll be changing the locks now, huh?'

He was right about changing the locks, and I would definitely be the only one with a key when we did. Jacques's story seemed pretty innocuous, so now I just had to find Sara and see what she had to say. Like the others, she told me what she'd been up to in the early hours of Thursday, and where she kept her keys.

"Wednesday night I had been with Martin, actually, finishing off a little bit of software we were developing. You know the one—the slow-burn worm that's harder to detect. We were at the storage facility until around eight p.m., which is unusual; I'm not normally there in the evening, but Martin wanted to work late and we were almost done, so we stayed later than usual. I had my key with me and offered to close up, but Martin likes to lock it up himself when he's leaving. I know he trusts me; I think it's just a habit. Anyway, I saw him lock it—it was definitely locked—and we both left with our own keys, so I haven't got much to help you with there.

"I got home about eight-thirty p.m., but I was feeling pretty wide awake. I made myself some spaghetti and then started working on a little side project of mine—a legit video game! It's still in the production stages, and it's just me messing about really, but I was doing that for a few hours. I knew Jacques and Leon were hanging out, but they must have been done by about eleven because I got a message from Jacques asking if I wanted to game—except he doesn't know that. I found him a few weeks ago on a new game I'd joined, and he doesn't know it's me he's been playing against; I figured it out a while ago, but I didn't want to say anything, and now I feel like it's almost too awkward to mention it. I didn't reply anyway, because I was still focusing on my own stuff, and I wanted to get some sleep.

"I probably slept from about midnight to three a.m., and when I came back online, I could see Jacques was gaming with someone

else, so he was obviously up too. I decided to go for a run—there was going to be a gorgeous sunrise—and I messaged the boys about it. Leon ignored me—he sleeps pretty heavily—but Jacques messaged back and said
he'd come. Our run actually went past Leon's place, so I knocked on the window to see if he was up. It's a bit antisocial, I guess, but I looked in through the one window and saw all the lights were off inside, so I guess he was still sleeping.

"We ran back to Jacques's place, and he made me an omelette for breakfast, which was cute—and then I was just leaving when the boss texted about the storage box. That must have been about seven a.m., and then you'll remember we got there just after you, about half an hour later. My key had been with me the night before, and I took it with me on the run. I never let it out of my sight, really. It's this one: right next to my house keys, see? So—I really don't get how this has happened.'

Sara's story seems trustworthy, and nothing really stands out; in fact, all three of the accounts seem to stack up, and I'm starting to wonder if we're following the right line of enquiry.

I start to try to put in a phone call to Martin to tell him what I've heard, but I know he's not going to be pleased—he wants answers, and he wants them soon. I'm put on hold, and after a few minutes of listening to the hold tone, I realize there's one small detail that doesn't sound quite right.

What's not adding up?

33. A Clean Sweep

You're a crime-scene cleaner for hire—on the side of the criminal.

Looking at this chaotic murder scene, can you spot the murder weapon that you've been employed to dispose of, and all the blood spatters you need to scrub away?

What is the murder weapon?

How many bloodstains are there to clean?

And why might the criminals have been interested in this room in the first place?

34. What a Wine-Up

A bottle of Château Margaux 1787 is up for auction and is expected to sell for $200,000 or more—but you've received a tip-off that it's a forgery.

Can you spot the clue on the label that makes certain that it's not the genuine vintage?

35. Grid Glitch

You have been busy coding up some hacking software with one of your technologically gifted colleagues. You're hoping it will give you access to the computers of those foolish enough to download and install it hidden inside pirated software, so that you can relieve them of any funds, passwords, and personal details they're trying to keep safe. You know—the usual sort of stuff.

Of course, you have to be careful when you're making malware— you don't want to let it loose on your own devices in case it ruins all your hard work so far.

Your colleague has created a three-digit code for you to unlock the software once it's safely on your own computer. He sends you a file supposedly containing the code, but when you open it, there seems to have been some sort of glitch—all that you can see on the screen are a series of pixelated grids.

What's going on? Have you accidentally activated the malware?

Just then, your hacker friend sends you a text. It says merely:

Left and right

At first you think this isn't much help at all, but when you look a little closer, you realize that these might be a clue to the code.

Can you work out what's going on with the glitched grids and discover the code to access the software?

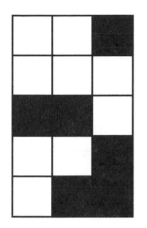

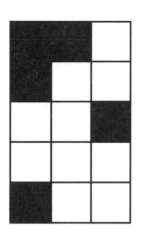

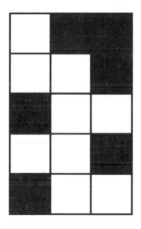

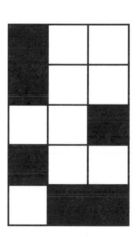

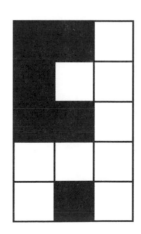

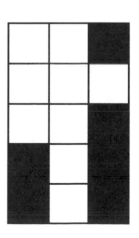

36. Signaling Code

You are lucky enough to have been working with one of the most advanced cybercriminals active today. It has been quite an apprenticeship, and he now thinks you might be ready to take on your first independent task.

When you ask when you'll be launching your next attack, his response is cryptic—he's learned how easily messages can be intercepted and doesn't take any chances.

```
technology is undoubtedly a gift. it keeps
us going. it's a wonder that only we truly
understand. but remember that the old ways
have their uses—keep an eye out for other
methods of communication from me—expect
the unexpected

you are making excellent progress. but don't
get complacent—and don't trust anyone—even
me—our enemies are learning as quickly as we
are—unfortunately

keep learning on your own—technology changes
as quickly as we can master it—an open mind
is the most important thing—don't take your
eye off the goal—remember everything you've
been taught—but don't write anything down
unless you want to get found out

watch out for other criminals who share our
expertise. there are some who would betray you
in a heartbeat. keep your friends close if you
have to. but it's better not to have friends.
much better.
```

the police should leave us alone
if they know what's good for them.
they know we can compromise their
network — and their security system — more
easily than they would like — so at least we
have that going for us

make sure you have a secure base when you
set up on your own — do not tell anyone
where you are working from - keep a physical
address — and ip address — under lock and
key — metaphorically of course

the final job i will ask you to do is a risky
one, but the reward is high. you will be
targeting a highly protected system. this
letter holds all the information you need to
work out when to go — although you may need
to look elsewhere for information to help you
decode the clues — i've always been more of a
traditionalist myself - it keeps the authorities
on their toes anyway

remember to keep calm once you have gained
access. your coding skills are second to none.
take anything that looks like it could be useful
to us — payment will be settled once the job is
complete - have fun with it — they won't know
what's hit them since they ain't no inspector
Morse

Can you work out the exact date (day, month, year) of your big
break from this email?

37. Red Ruby Robbed

The forger is one of the best in the business. He's been working on this replica of these nineteenth-century jewels for the best part of two

years—*precision* is his middle name. But he's missed out some key details from his diamond and ruby jewelry replica. Can you spot the mistakes? There are five differences between these two otherwise identical necklaces.

38. The Drone

You've just got your hands on some new drone technology, which you're hoping to use in your surveillance.

With the use of thermal imaging, the drone can create accurate blueprints and floor plans of a building from a bird's-eye view, meaning it's the perfect tool to help you map out the HQ of a criminal gang you've been tailing for a long time.

This particular ring is known for stealing small but valuable artworks, and selling them much later when it's harder to keep tabs on what's missing.

You think you've located their warehouse where they're keeping several masterpieces and want to get an idea of the scale of their storage. You might be in for a big raid, and you want to make sure you bring enough people with you.

The drone doesn't seem to be fully functioning, however—when you get the first set of data back, the measurements of the floor plan are incomplete.

You want to know the area of the whole building, but not all of the area has been calculated. You can see that the there are three rooms, and one of them—the midsized room—is a perfect square.

Can you work out the area of the largest room shown on the plan, indicated by the question mark?

Drone Feedback: Incomplete

Total Area: Unknown

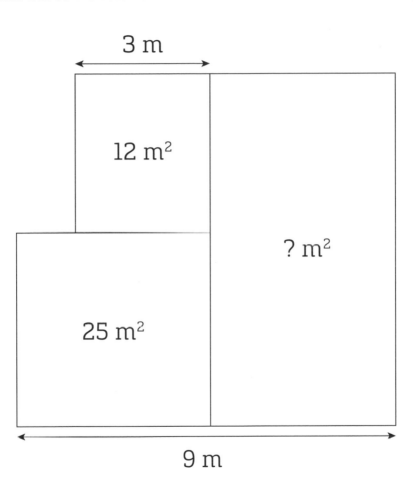

3 m

12 m²

25 m²

? m²

9 m

39. Caught Red-Handed

You've been tracking a criminal nicknamed Red Robin since you joined the force—although he had evaded capture for at least a decade prior to that.

He's been getting sloppy lately and has left behind five partial fingerprints, as shown below.

Your boss is putting you to the test... Are you up to it? Can you work out exactly how these five fragments connect to make a larger fingerprint?

40. Getaway Car

You've had a tip-off from the bank about the getaway car in which some criminals fled a bank heist, but the bank teller was so terrified they couldn't remember the whole license plate. All they could recall is the following:

Can you match the partial license plate to any of the cars below that are currently registered somewhere in the country?

RT60 CON   RT06 ONN   RT65 CNN
RT55 CON   RT56 OCN   RT60 OCN
RT06 OON   RT05 6CN   RT65 NON
RT65 CON   RT05 CON   RT05 CCN
RT60 5CN   RT50 OCN   RT56 OON
RT55 CCN   RT50 CON   RT65 OCN
RT55 CNN   RT65 C6N   RT05 CNN
RT06 OCN   RT65 NCN   RT60 CCN
RT60 CNN   RT05 CON   RT06 CON

41. Cyber Scams

You're an experienced cybercriminal, and for the last few years you've been working alone—with small-scale phishing operations, there's less motivation for the authorities to investigate you, as it's harder to pin down exactly how you work. On the surface, the damage you cause seems pretty minimal and not worth looking into—although the people you've scammed out of their life savings might say otherwise.

You've had an idea for a new scam to get people to share their passwords, but you think you'll need an assistant this time.

To set it up, you'll need someone to design a convincing set of web interfaces that look like genuine websites, so that victims will enter their details without getting suspicious. That way, you can gather all kinds of information about them, and then the choice is simply this: drain their accounts now, or drain them later.

To pull off this kind of project, you need someone who pays attention to the fine details—as stupid as your victims are, you don't want to give them reason to doubt your apparently squeaky-clean website. Everything has to look just right, and you want someone meticulously hardworking to help you create it.

You have contacted some trusted fellow scammers to see if they know anyone who would both be interested and suitable, and have gathered a list of potential candidates.

Your name commands quite a bit of respect in these circles so, when you introduce yourself to the people on the list, they all want to hear more about this project.

You get each interested party to send you a short message about their recent work, and their most impressive projects to date:

DaLLaS21 says: My best-ever scam went better than my wildest dreams—I was pretty selective about my targets, following them on social media, and then eventually managed to sign each and every one up to a pyramid scheme I'd designed.

It all looked pretty flawless—and this was a decade ago when social media was really taking off. I called it HighLights.

All these semisuccessful celebrities were signing up, hyped up about being successful entrepreneurs and business owners. We only took small payments from them at first, spreading them out so that nobody caught on. They were, however, able to say they were part of the growing business.

I worked with others already. I employed a girl from the very beginning to help me design the original platform—she was a website designer and I loved her work.

She helped me design a load of fake related websites too, to try to point more people towards HighLights. She was with me for about three years. Only thing is, just after she left, the police shut it down—although I like to think that's a coincidence.

I took a little career break—I'd made a fortune and didn't need to come up with anything new any time soon. So I took a few years out—four, in fact—and traveled the world.

Since then I've been working with the kid who set up Wormhole—a very smart kid. We're about to start working on something pretty cool—it's a combination of our skills, let's say—but I'd drop it in a heartbeat if I knew you had something special lined up.

You're impressed by these credentials—everyone's heard of HighLights—so you know you'll be keeping this candidate in mind. Your next applicant is someone you've never heard of, but has some very interesting work on their CV...

HintHint404 says: I started out as a security guard—nothing exciting, watching cameras mainly—until I figured out how they all worked as a system—and then how I could manipulate them.

I played around with some of the buildings I worked in, opening automatic doors, safes, and whatnot... I spent a year or so learning how to get into different systems undetected, and then how to do it from home.

Once I'd proved I could work for them remotely, I worked as a tech guy for a pretty notorious gang—I started four or so years ago now, and it was pretty low-risk for me. They'd find me a target—usually a bank or an auction house—and I'd disable the security remotely, leaving them to take what they liked.

I stopped doing that after about two and a half years—they were good to me, but they wanted to change their tactics and move into cybercrime a little more, so they didn't need any help with real heists on the ground.

I took a six-month break—it made sense to lie low for a while—and then I set up a little system with GamerGirl, and made ourselves a fake cybersecurity firm.

That's been going for a year now. She'd been working for the guy who set up HighLights—she started two years before I set up with the gang, so she'd been around a little longer and knew the ropes.

At the moment, I crack the systems, and she makes our security services look legit, and she's very good.

I'm not sure how loyal she is—I know she set up another rival company a while after she left HighLights—but at the moment we're making good money. What are you offering?

Seems like everyone knows everyone in the underground world. Next up, `GamerGirl` herself has applied for the position:

`GamerGirl` says: I was a website designer for a long time: all aboveboard, all squeaky clean. I was making pretty good money from it too, but it just wasn't fulfilling enough.

I got approached by the guy who was setting up HighLights, and it seemed like a pyramid scheme from the off, but he never asked for any money and promised me a cut, so I designed that interface for him, and, yeah, we made a mint. He started that six years ago, and I left three or so years after that, just before the police shut it down.

As soon as I quit, the kid who created Wormhole got in touch. I started working with him, helping him gently take money from his subscribers while hiding the transactions like we had with HighLights—but that all ended when he shut Wormhole down a year later.

Then I set up a kind of rival scheme to HighLights—the police trail had died down, and I swept up some of the more gullible former members, getting them to make different payments on shiny new websites.

I carried that on for a year, but it wasn't that fulfilling either, so for the last year I've been working with a guy with a background in building security. We made ourselves look like a legit cybersecurity business, showing up at corporations to rescue their networks after a "ransomware hack'—not knowing that we'd hacked them in the first place.

I made us a legit-looking website, branding, you name it, and then we'd get them to sign up to us: essentially we spooked them by taking some money illegally, opening some safe boxes remotely, publishing sensitive data we'd taken, whatever—and then got them to pay our "cybersecurity' firm real money to protect them from it.

He goes by HintHint404—he'll give me a reference if you need one. Like I say, we've been doing that for a year, and it's working pretty well—but I'm interested in what you have to say, in case you have something more exciting lined up.

She's certainly had an interesting career! Last in your lineup is someone whose reputation speaks for itself:

TOBI45 says: I started out with video games. I was a huge gamer and decided to design a few of my own, just for fun. I made a few small things, and then when I was fifteen—six years ago—I created Wormhole, and that was definitely my greatest success story so far.

I designed the whole thing: the graphics, the story. There were only four levels to start with, but nobody knows that—I just kept blocking everyone's progress while I created the later levels.

Eventually I made people sign up to get help—they didn't know I'd bugged the last six levels, so they were impossible to get through unless they paid me a hefty sum for the "hints'—which were bogus, and I was just unlocking levels for them in real time.

You probably know of the game, but it was crazy successful and had my real name attached to it, so I had to go underground if I wanted to make any serious money.

I gave up Wormhole four years after I started it, but I took those precious payment details with me. I helped myself every now and again, from different accounts; nobody got too suspicious.

In fact, for the final year of Wormhole, I got someone to help me out with it—she was good at disguising herself online and managed to make our charges look totally legit, so we got away with bigger and bigger amounts before I decided to shut the whole thing down. She was great though—goes by the name of `GamerGirl`, which I like to think is a tribute.

Since shutting down Wormhole, I've been working with the guy who set up HighLights—we'd started our previous scams around the same time, and we were ready to go again. We're about to start working on something pretty special, in fact—but I'm interested in what you're offering. I reckon we'd make a good pair.

In your line of work, it's not always easy to know who to trust, and you're always coming across people who are more than a little flexible with the truth.

Naturally, you refuse to employ anyone who is dishonest to you, and notice some discrepancies in the statements of your potential cooperatives.

One of the hackers seems to be hugely exaggerating to you, based on contradictions with what the others have said—but which one?

42. Money, Money, Money

An amazing horde of ancient coins has just been handed in to a top London auctioneer for valuation, but you've had to step in because the experts there think that one of the coins must be a forgery.

The classification assigned to each coin, based on previous coin discoveries, is shown alongside. But there is an historical anachronism on one of the coins. What is it?

**Greek gold Stator
350–300 BC**

**Medieval
Henry VI**

Roman
Hadrian

Greek
479–336 BC

Greek, Athens
c. 460 BC

43. Cryptic Counsel

You've been investigating a cybercriminal that you're sure is using cryptocurrency to launder money online.

So far you've linked three bank accounts to your suspect, but you know they're moving illegal funds into only one of these accounts.

You need to work out which one it is—and how much money is in it—before you carry out any more risky online surveillance.

One day, you receive an anonymous tip via email:

Your man has three accounts, and I know which account the illegal funds are in.

Each account has a nice whole number of millions in it.

The product of the three amounts in the accounts is $36m.

The total sum of all three accounts, in millions, is the same as today's day of the month.

You think about what the options are, but then you realize he hasn't given you enough information to work it out. You ping a message back:

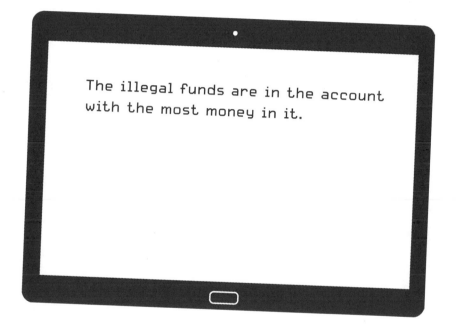

> I can't work it out from that! I need more info.

After a pause, your source sends a new email:

The illegal funds are in the account with the most money in it.

Aha! Now you have all the information you need to work out your answer.

How much is in the account that has the crypto-laundered money?

And what's today's day of the month?

44. Camera Clues

You're involved in a heist, with the aim of stealing some precious artifacts from a museum. However, to achieve this, you need to disable the CCTV system.

You have managed to break into the security control room, but have discovered that you need to type in a number-based password before you can access the camera controls. The only clue you can find is a cryptic message pinned on the noticeboard:

42 – 19 – 23 – 7 – 9

31 – 45 – 2 – 18 – 4

62 – 4 – 17 – 10 – 7

28 – 40 – 9 – 8 – 15

19 – 53 – 3 – 7 – 23

Password is the odd one out—something doesn't add up!

Can you work out which string of five numbers is the numerical passcode—before someone finds out what you're up to?

45. Hidden in Plain Sight

A drug cartel is aiming to import $5 million worth of class-A drugs at the end of this week. Your team has been waiting for the perfect in, and you've just been given it: their delivery driver has suddenly dropped dead. You're being drafted quickly to become their driver…but it's essential that you memorize your backstory so they believe you.

You have two minutes to read the information below and see if you can remember it after some questioning. Remember: wrong details cost lives.

- Your name is Arthur Gabriel Batelli

- Your father is Italian; your mother is Scottish

- You grew up in Liverpool, but moved to Dallas when you were eleven years old

- You went to prison when you were twenty-four years old for stealing a motorbike

- Prison was where you first met the gang leader of the drug cartel: Harry Brown

- Your fee for transporting the drugs will be $7,500

- You will be paid one third of the money when you pick up the drugs, and the rest on delivery

Make sure you read the information on the previous page before you answer these questions.

You jump in your car—and you're surprised to be joined by a passenger who's one of the gang. He's got a lot of questions for you, and it's time to remember who you're supposed to be. Can you recall these details of your backstory without letting slip that you're a mole?

1. What's your surname?

2. What's the name of the cartel's boss?

3. Where is your mother from?

4. How old were you when you stole the bike that got you locked up?

5. How much will you be paid in your first installment, after the initial pickup?

6. Where did you first grow up?

46. The Brothers Talk

You're a new member of a notorious crime syndicate run by three brothers who you have heard have very different approaches from the people they work with. One of the brothers always tells the truth, the second always lies, and the last brother is indecisive—he sometimes lies, but is occasionally honest.

You have made some notes during conversations with the three. Can you work out which brother is which, to get you off to a good start as part of the gang?

Marco:
"Alessandro is the indecisive one. I never know what he's really thinking. Sometimes he lies; sometimes he doesn't.'

Alessandro:
"No one ever really knows if Mateo is lying or telling the truth. He does both. It's quite a good trick really, keeps everyone on their toes.'

Mateo:
"Alessandro sometimes tells the truth, if it suits him, but don't put it past him to lie to you.'

47. Road Less Traveled

The bank robbery has just gone down, and now you need to get back to your hideout—stat!

The cops are onto you and are sure to be keeping an eye on all the main roads around the area. You're going to have to be clever.

Can you find the perfect escape route back from the bank to your hideout?

Here's what you need to do:

- Avoid all of the main roads. These are the wider roads on the map.

- To clarify, you can cross *over* a main road, so long as you go *straight across it* (putting your foot down as you do!)—you can't travel along a main road at all, so staggered junctions across them are out.

- You can take as long a route as you like, so long as you get there in the end.

Can you draw your route on the map opposite?

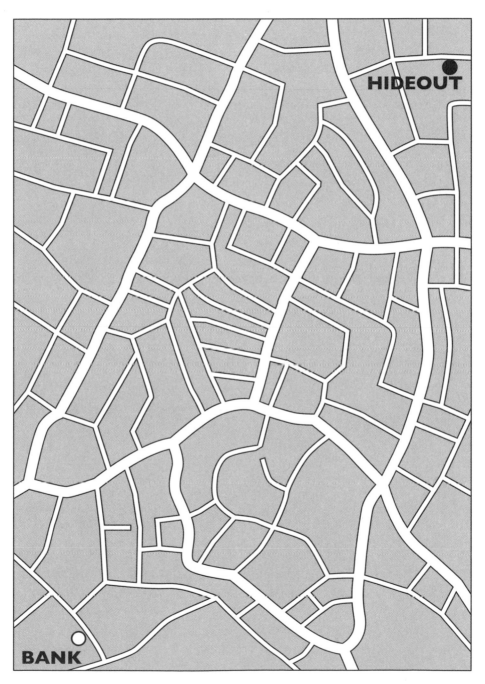

HIDEOUT

BANK

48. Friends on the Inside

You're serving time in prison, but luckily you have three friends who are helping you to plan your escape. They are sending you messages on a contraband phone that you can only occasionally check and can't use to send outgoing messages to query them.

Unfortunately, they are not great communicators, and the information you have received about the escape plan is a little unclear. Their messages are shown below.

See if you can use them to wwork out the plan, and make sure you're ready to run when the time comes.

- What time will the escape be?

- What exact date will the escape be?

- Which of the three gates will you use?

- Who is driving the getaway car?

A's messages:

It will be an afternoon this week (this week, starting Mon Jun 4)

I will cause a distraction during visitation—that's your chance to flee

I won't be driving

B's messages:

Front gate or back gate (not side gate)—not sure which

Not free at the weekend so won't be then— have told the others

C will open gate remotely but she'll have to stay inside after so not suspicious

C's messages:

Just got a badge. I'm in! My fake warden name is Phillips

Front gate double-guarded during visitation— can't use that

This week's visitations: Wed 10–11 a.m., Fri 3–4 p.m., Sun 2–3 p.m.

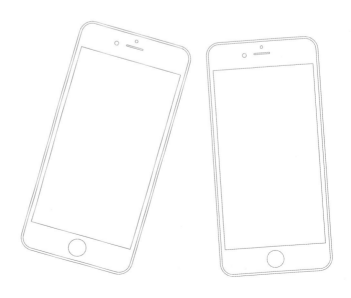

49. Hidden Treasure

Sometimes the old-school methods are the best. You have received a tip-off from your man on the inside that a gang specializing in jewel theft has ceased all electronic communication about where they hide their illegally acquired goods, instead favoring old-fashioned pencil and paper.

After seizing a briefcase from one of the suspected gang members, your colleague has managed to get his hands on a document that he believes will reveal the location of a bag of uncut diamonds recently stolen from a London jeweler.

The document appears to be a basic floor plan, but there's some crucial information missing—like where the walls are and the location of the diamonds. Perhaps it shows a property owned by a gang member?

Rifling through the briefcase, you find another strange document, as shown opposite.

In which room are the diamonds hidden?

Floor plan:

- Shade some squares according to the given clue numbers.
- The clues provide, in reading order from left to right or top to bottom, the length of every run of consecutive shaded squares in each row and column.
- There must be a gap of at least one empty square between each run of shaded squares in the same row or column.
- Solve and overlay.

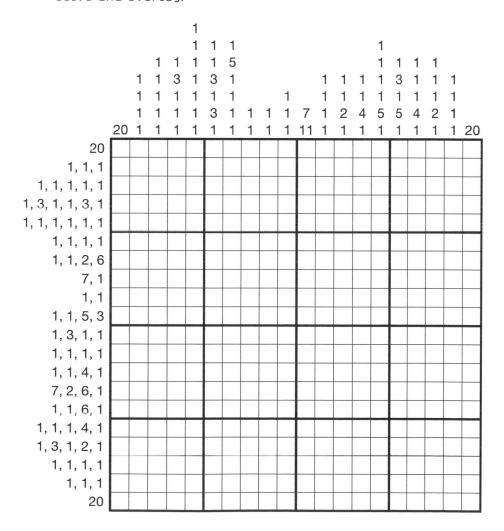

50. Snake in the Graph

You have built quite a niche for yourself in the criminal market, laundering money through your in-depth knowledge of computer games. You've built a good network with other gamers who tip you off on the latest info, and you are always looking out for the next big advance in gaming.

You are intrigued one day to see another gamer online, talking about a new game they have developed based on Snake. You download the game, and when you open it, a message flashes up on your screen:

<u>Rules and Regulations:</u>

Shade some squares to form a single snake that starts and ends at the given squares.

A snake is a path of adjacent squares that does not branch or cross over itself.

The snake does not bend back and touch itself—not even diagonally, except when turning a corner.

Numbers outside the grid specify the number of squares in their row or column that contain part of the snake.

Do you accept?

You choose yes, curious about how this new game will work. A grid pops up on the screen, on which you're clearly supposed to map out the path of the snake—and there are some numbers inside the grid too :

	6	5	2	3	5	3	3	5
5		1		2		3		4
2	5		6		7		8	
6		9		1		2		(H)
1	3		4		5		6	
6		7		8		9		1
4	2		3		4		5	
5		6		7		8		9
3	1		2		3	(T)	4	

Before you can get started, however, something else flashes up on the screen:

ENTER PASSCODE—OR I EMPTY YOUR ACCOUNTS

A countdown has started—and this suddenly doesn't seem like a game at all. Have you just met your match?

You need a numeric code to shut down the game before this mysterious programmer drains your bank accounts (or tries to).

Once the snake is complete, it will pass through several numbers in the grid: read them from the head (H) to the tail (T) of the snake to reveal the code.

51. Animal Instincts

Endangered animals can be worth a fortune on the black market.

You have had your eye on a nearby animal sanctuary for a while, and after careful planning have broken in.

You have managed to capture a lynx and a lemur, and have also picked up a sack of lemur food.

When you get back to your stylish two-seater sports car, however, you realize that you may not have fully thought this through, since you can only fit one of the three items—the two animals and the large sack of food—at a time into the passenger seat of your car.

Luckily you don't have far to go, so you decide you'll just need to make multiple trips. Luckily there's a disused shed just outside the sanctuary where you can leave the animals and the food temporarily out of sight, while you drive there and back.

The trouble is, however, that the lynx might attack the lemur if they are left alone, and the lemur will probably rip open its food sack if left alone with it. This will be true either here in the disused shed or back at your HQ, which is unmanned at the moment.

How can you transport both animals and the bag of food back to your HQ without any animals being chased away or the food being eaten? Remember you can only move one at a time between them.

52. Password-Protected

You have conducted a raid at the home of a prominent UK coding expert who has recently been implicated in a series of hacking incidents targeting the police.

The computer is (of course) password protected, but your guesses have failed, and you are in despair of ever unlocking it when you find a strange note in a drawer. It might be a clue to the password:

- START: at P (push)
- Left: 1 (push)
- Left: 5 (push)
- Right: 1 (push)
- Left: 4, down: 1 (push)
- Right: 8 (push — END)

Hint: the keys are at your fingertips

Can you make sense of the note to discover the password?

53. Valuable Pictures

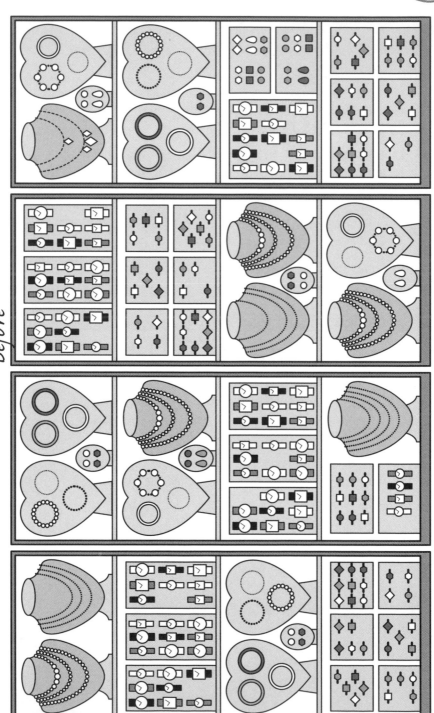

A gang has stolen ten valuable items from a famous jewelry store. You've just arrived on the scene and have been asked to compare before and after photos. Can you identify all ten missing items?

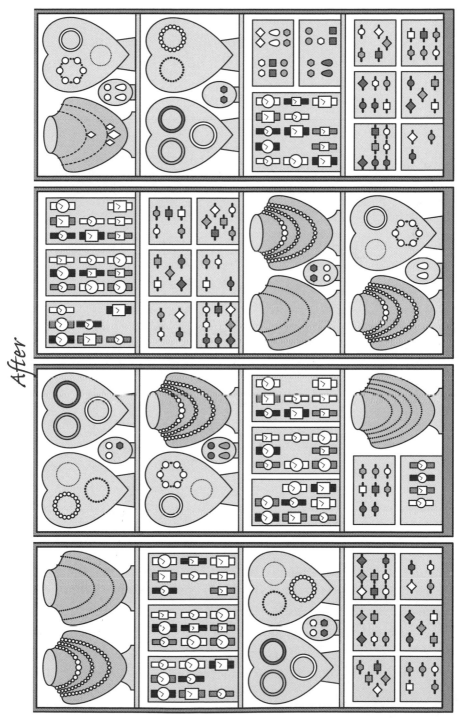

54. Membership Costs

You've been the head of a notorious crime ring for several years, and members have come and gone during your time as boss—some for good reasons, some for bad. It takes a long time to bring someone new into your confidence. You need your employees to prove that they're committed and smart—and won't lie to you.

Over the last year, you've had four new people start to work for you who have seemed trustworthy—at least until now. You have a hunch that one of them is really working undercover for the authorities, and your hunches tend to be spot on.

You don't want to spook any of the four new members, in case your mole gets cold feet and scarpers before you have a chance to show them what happens to anyone who crosses you.

You decide to speak to each of the new members in turn, making some small talk, and asking how their weekends were. You start with Mel, the youngest recruit of the four, and ask how she spent her time off:

> "Oh, it was good, you know. Friday night was pretty quiet. Went back to my apartment with a pizza after playing some cards with Sammy—he cleaned me out; he's a real card shark, took every bit of cash I had. Lucky the pizza guy is a friend, right?
>
> "Saturday morning I cleaned the windows at the back of my apartment—I had some neighbors making comments, and I don't need anyone talking about me and drawing attention to my place, looking into my windows when they should be minding their own business. Then I washed my car, which was a waste of time because it rained so much in the afternoon it would have done the job for me anyway.

"I gave Sammy a lift to the train station in the afternoon—I wish he'd just take some lessons and learn to drive because I'm getting sick of doing these favors, but he had to see his family, I guess. I later gave Sammy a lift home too, after midnight—we actually passed Anders and someone else in his scratched car on the way back. They were waiting at a red light in the lane next to me, but they didn't wave—losers!

"Sunday morning I went to my mother's and didn't leave until way after six—that woman likes to feed her guests, and I picked up a pretty good tan sitting out in her garden in the afternoon. And then some video games in the evening. How about you—a good weekend?'

You answer that your weekend was fine—and you don't let on that you've spent it wondering which of your members might turn out to be a traitor.

Flinn is next, who joined you on Friday night—so you know what he was doing then, at least:

"Well, Friday night I was with you—I probably got in around one a.m. once we finished. Saturday morning was super boring—spent an hour or so at the Post Office waiting for something my mother sent from home. International post is the worst, and I had places to be—well, a football game, specifically. That was good until it got rained out in the second half.

"Saturday night I went out for some food and spotted Anders coming out of the cinema with a guy I didn't know but turned out to be his brother. They invited me out for a drink with them, and Anders gave me a ride home, in his beat-up car—he really should take better care of it. I was home by eleven p.m.

"Sunday morning I got up late—just before noon—and then headed straight out to the park for a jog. I saw Sammy there in a Hawaiian shirt, not very subtle! I don't think he saw me in my running gear and sunglasses. It's a small park, small world. Then I went home, had a shower, made myself a lasagna, fixed my bike. It was all pretty good.'

Next up is Sammy; he and Mel joined at the same time:

"Saturday morning I was on the phone with the bank half the time—can't show my face in the building, but my card has gone missing, and I need to empty that account. Luckily I thrashed Mel at poker on Friday night, so I had something to tide me over for the weekend anyway.

"Saturday afternoon I took a train out west, saw some family, came back on the last train around midnight. Mel picked me up and took me home again—what a hero.

"Sunday morning was nice and relaxed—I went out to a bakery early and got a few pastries for the morning, sat out on my balcony in the sunshine watching the world. I wanted to make the most of the weather, so I threw on some shorts and a shirt and went to the park just before midday. I spotted Flinn there in full jogging gear: sweatbands, sunglasses on, the lot. He looked hilarious, but he's a nice kid.

"I picked up a milkshake on the way home and then watched a movie in the evening tucked up in bed. Wild weekend, huh? Did you get up to much after Friday night? Everything go to plan?"

Without revealing too much, you say that Friday night went well—which it did.

Finally, you ask Anders—who's been with you the longest of the four—how his weekend went:

"Nothing special, not much to report. Sammy and Mel had asked me if I wanted to play some poker with them Friday night but I bailed—I had a hot date lined up and didn't want to miss it.

"Saturday morning I went for a long run along the docks—got to keep that fitness up—and then dropped my car off at the garage sometime in the afternoon. They owed me a favor, so they had agreed to touch it up for free—it's been in a few scrapes recently, and I should keep it looking unremarkable.

"Saturday night I went to the movies with my brother and then we stayed out for a few drinks. Flinn joined us—he caught us coming out of the cinema, but we all left pretty early and I was in bed by midnight.

"Sunday morning I picked up the car—looking good as new from the garage—and drove over to the park. I needed the fresh air to clear my head a little. I left when the rain started, just after noon. I got home, did some laundry, hung it on the line, ate some spaghetti, and called my Grandma—nothing major. Everything go smoothly on Friday night?'

You reply—again without revealing too much—that everything went perfectly on Friday, and you head back to your office.

Someone is lying to you. Who?

55. Home Visits

An expert hacker who has been at large for a while has moved onto robbing the houses of the rich and famous by targeting and disabling their security systems. She has successfully completed several robberies, but has recently got cocky and started taunting you with clues as to who her future victims will be.

She's sent you a text message every day this week, and she's obviously done quite a bit of homework on these targets. You're hoping you can use the information she's sending to work out who she'll be targeting later today—so that you can meet her there with a pair of handcuffs.

Here's what she's sent you so far:

- Three Ms to watch out for—Maida Vale, Mayfair, Marylebone!

- The actor lives in a lovely terraced house, don't you think?

- Spotted a lovely detached place in Marylebone...

- That singer has a lovely apartment (with a rooftop bar)

• Your sports star doesn't live in Mayfair—surprised by that

• Shame that the place in Maida Vale is terraced. Does have a nice tennis court tho

• The one with the tennis court, the one with the pool, or the one with the rooftop bar? Decisions, decisions!

You've just received another message:

• Think I'll go for the place with the pool today!

Time to spring into action! What does their target do, where do they live, and in what kind of property?

56. Notable Deception

As a test of your abilities, you've been asked to pick out a forged banknote from this collection of otherwise genuine ones. Can you use your observation skills to successfully identify the forgery in the set of six bank notes on the opposite page?

You don't need any preexisting knowledge to solve this puzzle—just attention to detail.

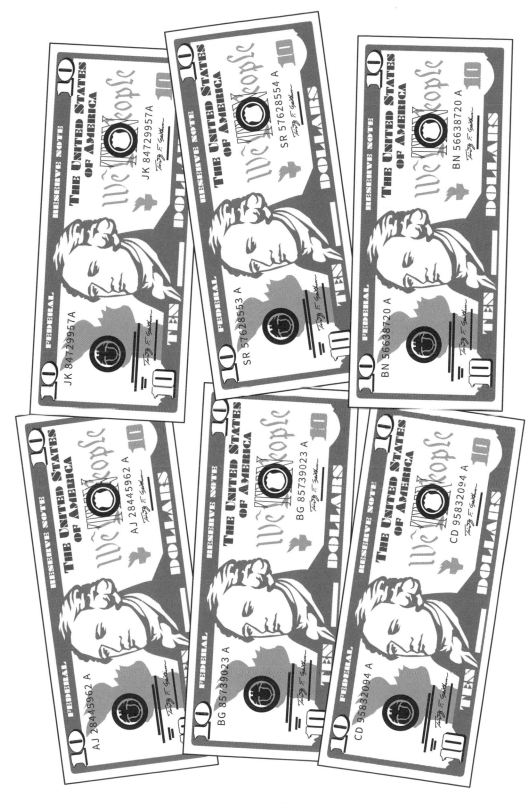

57. The Great Escape

You've been undercover investigating a drug cartel, and you had almost managed to get into the inner circle when they found you out. Now you're being held hostage while they wait for the higher-ups to decide what to do with you, and you're not sure you want to wait around to find out what happens next.

You think you might be able to escape if you can just time it well enough—there are six guards keeping watch on you in shifts, but they all tend to lose focus at the end of each of their time slots.

You'll need to work out the guard's rotations to figure out the next time they're all changing over at the same time, as that's your best chance of escape.

There are always three types of guards watching you. One type of guard swaps person on duty every two hours, another type of guard swaps person on duty every three hours, and the third type of guard swaps person on duty every three and a half hours.

Three guards, once of each type, have just started their shifts together—so the next time all three shifts swap over at the same time will be the time to make a run for it.

Taking the schedule into account, how many hours is it until you try to make your escape?

And seeing as you've got time on your hands to work it all out, how many times will each type of guard change shift from now until the shift change where you try to escape (including that shift change too)?

58. Go Phish

You and a friend are attempting to pull off a series of phishing scams and have gathered a list of people to target. Your friend has made a few preliminary phone calls and managed to gather some personal data about each target to use in convincing them of your honesty. However, he got careless and ended up being arrested.

You have recovered his notes, but it's up to you to unravel the facts about each person so you can pull off the scam.

- The person who works for the government will be contacted about their bank account

- The person to be scammed via snail mail will be contacted about their health insurance

- "MP' is a software engineer

- The retired postal worker will be phished via telephone call

- "ZN' will be contacted via email

- The person to contact about cryptocurrency should not be emailed

- "CJ' doesn't work for the government

Can you work out:

- What each person does for a living?
- How they'll be contacted?
- What they'll be contacted about?

59. Wormholes

You're a pretty big name in the world of cybercrime, but even you can't do everything on your own. You have managed to corrupt a young computer scientist who has developed a malware worm for you.

Unfortunately, the worm has got out of control, and the scientist has scarpered. Your hope was that you could use the worm to cause havoc online, but right now it's just destroying your own computers. You need to try and stop the damage.

Your HQ setup is made of five different computers, all linked together in daisy-chain formation. It was supposed to be more secure, isolating them from the internet, but it doesn't seem to have worked.

The worm is programmed to spread through them one by one, destroying all the data on one computer's hard drive before it moves onto the next. It starts off slowly and then speeds up—to ramp up the tension for the poor victim and encourage them to quickly pony up the cash for us to disable it before they lose *all* their data.

Unfortunately we haven't yet written the remote disable, so I'm going to have get into our office as fast as possible, before we lose all of our data.

In the first fifteen minutes, the worm will destroy 1TB of disc space. Then in the next fifteen minutes, it will destroy as much data as it did in the previous fifteen minutes *plus* another 2TB of data. This increase takes place every fifteen minutes. This means that after the second block of fifteen minutes—i.e. half an hour after it starts running—it will have destroyed 4TB of data: the first 1TB, then another 1TB again, plus the extra 2TB.

Here's how your devices are set up, including their storage capacities:

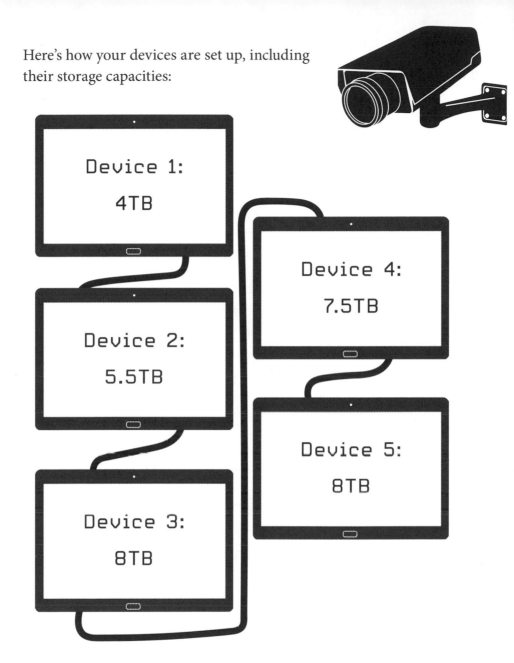

Device 1: 4TB

Device 2: 5.5TB

Device 3: 8TB

Device 4: 7.5TB

Device 5: 8TB

Device 5—the one that the worm will reach last—has all of your most private data on it, and you can't afford to lose that. From the moment the worm was released, how long will it take until it first starts destroying data on the fifth device?

If it will take you one and a half hours to get into the office, will you be there in time?

60. Catch the Virus

Disaster has struck—you have been emailing someone who claimed to have information about a case you are working on, but they turned out to be a cybercriminal!

A file they sent, claiming it contained damning evidence, actually contained ransomware, which has infected your computer. Whoever sent it is threatening to release the newly accessed classified information out into the world, so you have to act quickly.

Your computer expert has managed to find some information about where the attack is coming from, and they've pulled together a list of coordinates that give the possible geographical locations of the IP addresses they think belong to the suspect.

After a more thorough search through the coordinates, your expert manages to give you the following information on the location of the hacker:

- You can rule out the most northerly location

- The suspect's coordinates have both odd and even digits

- The suspect is in the northern hemisphere

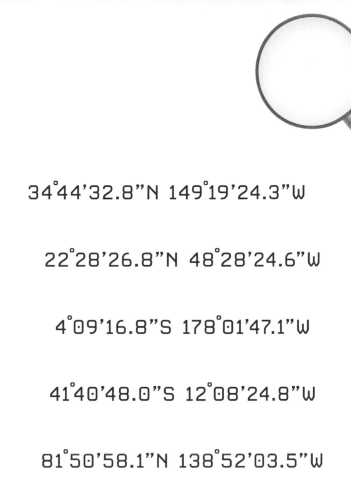

34°44'32.8"N 149°19'24.3"W

22°28'26.8"N 48°28'24.6"W

4°09'16.8"S 178°01'47.1"W

41°40'48.0"S 12°08'24.8"W

81°50'58.1"N 138°52'03.5"W

55°15'53.9"N 31°17'37.5"W

Can you work out which of the coordinates gives you the real location of your wanted criminal?

61. Identity Parade

It's time to test your observation skills again, with a practice identity parade that is being held at the station to test out all the new recruits.

Can you spot the pretend criminal in the lineup opposite, using the series of bullet-point descriptions below?

1. First, eliminate anyone who does not have the same tie on as at least one of the other suspects—or has no tie on.

2. Then, with the remaining suspects, eliminate the person who has a very different hairline from the rest.

3. Then remove the two people who have substantially different jacket colors from the others.

4. Next, remove the person whose tie has stripes in a different direction from the rest.

5. At this point, eliminate the person with different-colored hair from the remaining people.

6. You should now have three people left—two of which have almost identical facial appearances, who you can eliminate.

7. This leaves one person: the criminal.

After reading all of the clues, can you identify the correct person?

62. Burn After Solving

It's time to lie low for a while. Your mob boss has arranged for you to hide from the police after your latest showdown with a rival mob family, as you're wanted by a lot of people.

Your rivals have tapped your phone, so you'll have to resort to other methods of communication to make your getaway—unless you fancy a rematch.

Your boss has told you that you have to leave by plane, and she's sent you these notes to tell you which airport to go to. Looks like you'll have to be quick—there's a flight to catch!

Good work kiddo, you earned a break. Here's your hideout info, but remember to keep a low profile. You know the rules:

- **Shade some squares according to the given clue numbers.**

- **The clues provide, in reading order from left to right or top to bottom, the length of every run of consecutive shaded squares in each row and column.**

- **There must be a gap of at least one empty square between each run of shaded squares in the same row or column.**

You'll figure it out!

Where are you flying to today? Make sure you get rid of the evidence as soon as you know where you're going!

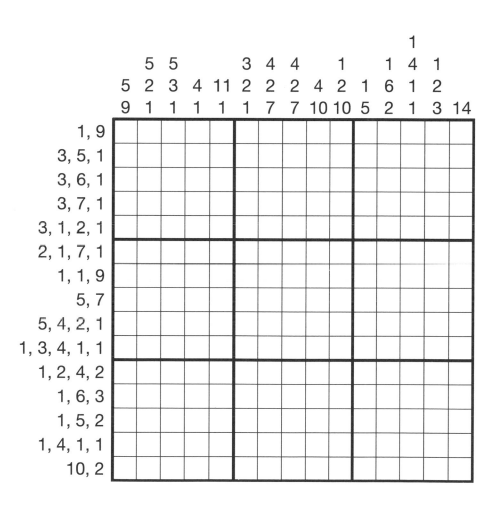

63. Don't Feed the Trolls

A well-known TV personality recently approached you, complaining of difficulties with three social media trolls. You have managed to gather various pieces of information about the names and whereabouts of the perpetrators from their comments online.

Can you use your notes to pin down the real names of the trolls and the cities they live in, so you can get in touch with the relevant authorities?

What is each troll's real name, where do they live, and on what platform are they posting?

- rude_hanna is not the one trolling on Twitter

- Sam Bennet is the real name of 80schild

- The person in Buenos Aires is trolling on Instagram

- Tiny247 is posting on Facebook

- Luc Dune lives in London

- Anna Hermosa doesn't use numbers in her online name

- The person trolling on Twitter lives in New York City

64. Stroke of Genius

You are hatching a plan to "fly' one of your associates out of prison. They have managed to learn the six-digit access code for the online security system, which they want you to then disable.

Your associate has acquired a phone, but their texts are being monitored by other inmates keen to get in on the plan. They have concealed the code in a series of text messages:

> You will soon have everything
> you need for the flight
> info (which is key boarding
> information)
>
> Remember to pay attention to
> details & question everything!
>
> 99% of the time in life you will
> be taken more seriously if you
> pay attention to punctuation
>
> Remember that your reward will
> be $100000
>
> Now unshift yourself and get
> going

There are three clues in the messages as to what to do. Can you spot the keywords and deduce the six-digit code?

65. Tattoo Terror

You think you might have just apprehended a member of a particularly notorious criminal gang.

Members of this gang are known for having exact replicas of one of the symbols shown below tattooed somewhere on their torsos.

Can you match one of these symbols to the gang member's torso, shown opposite?

66. Track the Tracks

You have received a call to the control room of a busy underground train network. A hacker has infiltrated their communication system and changed the numeric access code. You don't know what they're planning, but this doesn't seem like good news—and you're pretty sure that disaster is imminent.

Your IT experts let you know that they have discovered a mysterious grid left by the hacker, which is now flashing up on the screen. At first it seems like a partial map of the track system, but when you look a little closer, there are some numbers dotted across the area—and plenty of pieces of track missing.

	7	1	1	2	4	5	3	2
4		1		2		3		4
3	5		6		7		8	
3		9		1		2		3
3	4		5		6		7	
3	▦	8		9		1		2
5	3		4		5		▦	
3	◈	6		7		8		9
1	1		2		3	▦	4	

As you look more closely at the image, words begin to appear underneath—it looks like the hacker is typing out a message to you in real time:

All aboard the chaos train!

I'm playing fair—you have a chance to reveal the new passcode and take control of the tracks again. Hope you've got a sharp mind and a sharp pencil!

The train will enter the left-hand column and leave at the bottom row—and I've also left two other pieces for you. It'll travel around this area, but it won't leave the grid otherwise, and it won't cross its own path. Promise.

I'm feeling generous, so I've left a bunch of clues: numbers outside the grid reveal the number of track pieces in each row and column. And you know the track: only straight sections and right-angled turns.

The track path will cross over several numbers in the grid. Read the numbers in the order of the train's journey, and you'll get your precious code back. You have ten minutes to get everything back on track— and then I'll start moving things around for real. So good luck!

What's the new code?

67. Message in a Bottle

The boss is on a kidnapping spree, abducting five people in as many days. Each time he leaves a bottle behind, as a little present to the police who come to investigate the scene of the crime long after he's gone.

Being the kindhearted man he is, the boss has left some clues on the bottles. We doubt the police will work them out, but if they have the smarts, then at least they'll have one chance to get back the five people without any unnecessary unpleasantness. You can't say fairer than that, can you?

The five bottles the boss is dropping off—one per day—are shown opposite.

I've taken a look at them, and I worked it all out—and I wouldn't say I was the smartest cookie in the toolbox. Although I did have a few hints from the boss, if I'm being honest.

Without any hints at all, can you find out how to recover the five people?

ADESTUY
PEOPLE
IN
HOTEL

ADFIRY
ARE
TWENTY
STREET

ADDEENSWY
YOU
ROOM
PARADISE

ADMNOY
THE
HIDDEN
SEVEN

ADHRSTUY
SEEK
NUMBER
NEW

68. A Date for Your Diary

You have been tracing a criminal gang renowned for leaving clues at their crime scenes, giving detectives hints as to where they are planning to target next.

You're pretty fed up with their taunts, but you have to play their game if you want to beat them to the next location.

You have discovered the following clue at one of their latest break-ins:

Disregard everything you find in THIS CLUE

LEBCATIRHSNS EBSLAUTRCT HLDIOICOLHSRTMUEAHINST

Soon you realize it's not a place at all, but has details about a person you can contact to find out more about the organization.

Who is it, and where do they work?

69. The Newcomer

You have recently accepted a new recruit into your gang, but are becoming increasingly unsure as to where their loyalties lie.

You have "borrowed' their phone to see if they have been speaking to anyone outside the gang. You notice they've had an upgrade: they used to use an old-school Nokia.

You find a series of text messages, but rather than words, they are just strings of numbers:

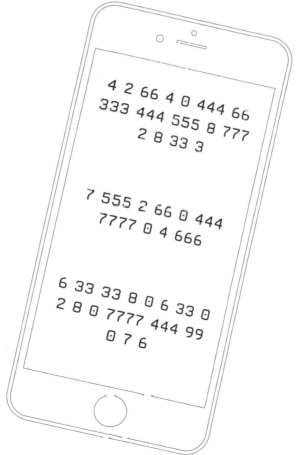

What is their plan?

70. Rubbish Job

You've drawn the short straw and are searching a bin near the crime scene for clues. Can you find the discarded murder weapon hidden in among all the rubbish?

71. All Blocked Up

Can you find a way across town with your hostage while avoiding crossing the police roadblocks, marked with Xs?

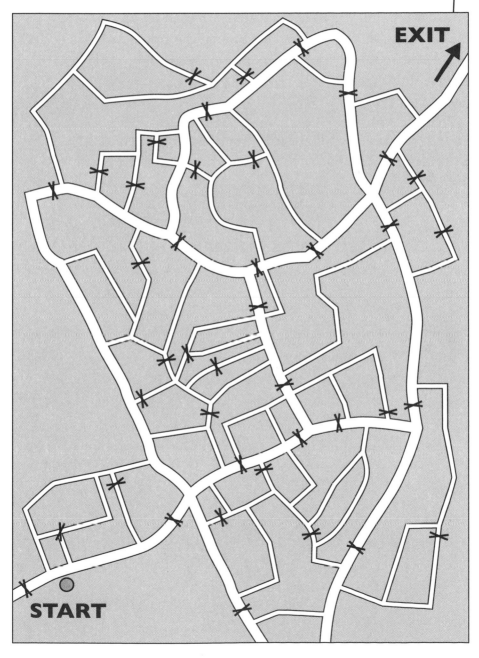

72. Crack the Code

As the leader of an infamous criminal gang, you have to cultivate an air of power and control.

To help with this, you have decided to introduce a series of tests for new recruits. You have told the wannabe criminals to crack into a safe without using force of any kind. Of course, you don't need to do all the hard work yourself, so you draft someone in to create the test.

Your colleague has written a mysterious message containing clues and sent it to you to check before the challenge begins.

counting capital totals

the first thing to remember is that ALL money we make must be sent to our trusted Laundering Partners before it can be logged as "Income'

wages are frequently reviewed. do NOT expect that you will earn the same as others. build trust over time, and Work Your Way up

our HQ (located in London) holds all our Administrative Records, so the location must be kept secret at ALL costs

all income earned through
Fraud, Robbery, Blackmail,
Abduction, Violence, etc must
be declared immediately—
anyone found in possession of
undeclared assets will suffer
"punishment'

we are not the only crew in
the area, so all cash, jewels,
and other valuables must be
stored in our safe. The code
is now in your possession, so
you just have to find it... Read
each paragraph of this email
carefully since there's one digit
hidden in each—the subject line
tells you how

Your colleague has done a good job, and the test is ready for the recruits.

What is the five-digit code to the safe? As a clue, the first digit is 6.

73. Got Your Number

It is always astounding how often criminals feel the need to "sign' their deeds in some way.

You have arrived at a crime scene to investigate the murder of a man in his study. While going through the papers on the desk, you find a bloodstained sheet of paper with a series of numbers written on it, taped to the table. Clearly someone wants you to see it.

Your officers have already collected the names of four people who were near the scene of the crime, and they're your main suspects at the moment.

12 15 15 11   6 15 18   20 8 5

16 5 18 19 15 14   23 9 20 8   20 8 5

9 14 9 20 9 1 12 19   1 3

ABCDEFGHIJKLMNOPQRSTUVWXYZ

You're sure this note will reveal that one of the four is involved, if only you can work out what it means.

Four suspects:

Monica Llewellyn

Daniel Aldershof

Aitana Clemensen

Lottie Constable

Can you work out, from the list of suspects and the bloodstained note, who committed the murder?

74. Binary Bust

You have been having trouble intercepting communication between criminals recently and have discovered that a local crime organization has been using online game chat rooms to make their plans. You have created a character for yourself and managed to engage them in a conversation—but suddenly their messages stop making sense and become a jumble of characters. You can't crack the code in time, but you manage to take a picture of three lines of text:

A1T7M4G5WRH

56GTA7NR34KED 3XD907UAS 2NMLO500R4DQ

3P1TA60GR2IHST

The letters disappear from the screen—good job you took a photo—and are suddenly replaced by binary code. At first you think it might be an error message caused by a glitch in the game, but then you look closer:

01010101001

00101001000010 001000100 010010001010

01001000101010

That code is trying to tell you something. Can you work out what is going on, and where to find the criminals?

75. Internet Infiltrator

You have been sent on a risky mission—to break into the house next door and steal their Wi-Fi passcode so you and the other felons you live with can stop paying for yours.

When you get there, all you discover is a piece of paper pinned to the wall with a few clues on it—can you use the clues to work out the code?

Remember:

passcode is numbers only!

[Error: HTTP Page Not Found] [All the time] [A baker's dozen] [Famous secret agent] [Call in a USA emergency]

[_ _ _][_ _ / _][_ _][_ _ _][_ _ _]

76. Note to Self

Any cybercriminal worth their salt knows not to write passwords down. But with so many complex heists and covert operations on the go, your head is full of other things, and you have been finding yourself forgetting them more easily. You made yourself a note to help you remember the six-digit password to get into your boss's laptop, but now you have forgotten even how that works. Can you work out the code before he arrives?

Only the words in the central column are in the wrong order—restore the pairs to reveal the correct numbers! Remember, look at endings before beginnings, always read left to right, and only 1–9 are used. Each entry is used exactly once.

MARTINI	THUNDER	(2, 2)
COLLUSION	WORKSHOP	(2, 1)
APPLAUSE	OURSELVES	(2, 3)
HINDSIGHT	NEWSPAPER	(1, 2)
SLEIGH	ENGINE	(4, 1)
WOLF	VENGEANCE	(1, 3)

77. Phone a Friend

You have hired an expert in identity fraud to help you create a series of fake social media accounts that you can use as a cover for the schemes you have planned.

You need to speak with the expert, but sharing phone numbers is a risky business since neither of you wants to fully release your phone number, or at least be the first one to do it.

Your expert has relented and has now sent you an email with the information you need—but first you need to work out how it has been hidden.

Subject:
First things first - phone number

Message:
Seems even virtual extorters need to watch out. For our undercover representatives, new information naturally emerges - ferret out uninformed reps. They have restricted efficiency. Evaluate our notable emissaries - find informants. Vet everyone thoroughly: watch, observe. Fraudulent operations undo resolutions.

What is the hidden phone number?

78. High-End Burglary

You've lurked outside a town house until the owners have left for the evening, and now you're inside.

Can you spot the highest-value items in the living room that it is sensible to make off with?

Which is likely to be the one item that will cause the least suspicion if you're searched on the way out, but represents probably the highest value?

79. Unreliable Witness

You have taken a crime-scene photograph:

An eyewitness to the burglary has told you what they saw at the time of the crime, but something seems off. Following your detective instincts, can you find the inconsistency in the witness statement?

> "I was just home from work yesterday evening when I heard a window smash next door. I went outside—and spotted a burglar through the window of my neighbor's house! They were emptying out the drawers, knocking over mugs, and scattering pens and pencils everywhere. I'm not sure what they were looking for, but they even emptied the wastepaper basket. It was complete chaos. That's when I called the police, but the burglar spotted me and fled the scene before you arrived."

80. A Risky Experiment

A murder has taken place in a laboratory at a pharmaceutical company, and the technician has been poisoned, although it's not clear what with.

You look around the room. There's an unusual chart pinned up on the wall, but it doesn't seem to tell you anything useful:

	A	B	C	D	E	F	G
5	L	D	Q	D	C	B	A
4	G	S	A	W	S	U	M
3	R	L	F	A	G	V	E
2	N	P	A	Y	V	E	Z
1	I	O	B	F	T	X	I

Just as you're about to give up hope, you spot a small note by the door.

Whoever wrote the note seems to have listed what looks like four chemical substances—but when you look closer, you think the symbols might be telling you something else.

In fact, now you're sure this is giving you a hint to the murderer's identity.

- $C_4A_2D_3$

- B_5F_2

- B_3C_2

- $E_4G_3A_5F_3G_5$

Can you work out who to arrest from the clues?

81. What the Spies Say

You and your team have been investigating a mysterious international intelligence agency that seems to be operating on the wrong side of the law.

It appears to be a group that passes information between major crime syndicates while keeping an eye out for any official organizations that might try to bring those syndicates down from the inside.

You have made contact with the agency and are now trying to infiltrate their ranks. Before they hire you, however, they need to make sure that you're as observant as you claim you are. They say they can't take any risks with new recruits.

You receive an email from the leader of the organization, and you're told it contains a hidden message. Is the subject line a clue?

Subject: Retrieve NATO letters

Our business model takes some time to understand fully—we don't just hire anyone, however good their credentials, so we have decided to send you on a simple mission to see what you can do. You have a reputation as an agent who's careful, enterprising, and sympathetic to our cause—but keep in mind that we are watching, and this is your chance to spell it out to us.

We have been laying the groundwork for this mission since last November, so all you should need to do is carry out the final steps and pick up the documents. The documents we need are hidden in a filing cabinet in the NATO building, and you will gain access to it as a special delivery worker who's carrying a package for a member of senior management. Everything is organized, and the plan should work, but be careful—NATO has eyes and ears everywhere, and if they get a heads-up that they are playing host to a charlatan, God help you.

The building itself is something of a fortress—once you have used your fake documentation to breach the walls of this citadel, take special care to examine your surroundings so you can find your way out. Your uniform (which we will send to you soon) should mean that few will question you, but getting lost could jeopardize your cover story, as the delivery person you are impersonating knows the building like the back of his hand. When you get to the filing cabinet containing the documents, work quickly, but pay attention, and do not mess it up—apart from anything else, any mistakes here will mean the end of our association. Remember, we chose you for your skills in exactly this area, but you have to prove yourself capable.

Once we have made it clear that we are in possession of the main dossier, ramifications for NATO will reveal themselves, and they will be severe. If you pull this off, it will be quite a feather in your cap—a pay-off for your hard work so far. In terms of next steps, we are sending you a package that will contain diagrams of the building—make sure to study these in detail. As you will discover, once you are inside, you will have three choices of routes to get to the filing cabinet. I'll sign off for now—we will organize a meeting before long, and it will be easier raising any questions in person.

What's the hidden message?

82. Double Agent

Your boss is agitated. He's just been told that there's a potential mole in your criminal network: an undercover police officer hiding among the ranks. The police seem to have always been one step ahead of you for the last few months, which must be because they're getting information from the inside.

Luckily, your boss has his *own* moles, who have found a copy of the letter the police commissioner sent to the suspected undercover agent, instructing them as to what name to use while in the gang. If you can find out their alias, you can confront them head-on.

For security reasons, the name has been disguised—but you're pretty sure you can crack the code. If you're the one who manages to unmask the traitor, then you might just put yourself in line for a promotion.

> Dear Agent X,
>
> I am so glad you suggested infiltrating this group, since it is going to be quite a coup for our team when we take their leader into custody. In fact, I think the interrogation might end up being the highlight of my working life. But you need to be careful—they won't trust you straightaway. Take your time settling into the gang, and make sure they think of you as one of their people before you take any action. Aaron is going to be your main point of contact here, since you have worked together many times, and I trust him with the task.

As for your undercover name, only those who absolutely must know it should have it—it becomes a tricky business otherwise. We must avoid you getting into trouble. Good thing we have a system already for hiding such things—just search for the name in the usual way. Try to get into the inner circle of the group if you can, since it should be easier to find things out if you are trusted. Everyone here agrees that you are the best chance we have.

Yours sincerely,

Fiona

P.S. A hint in case you can't remember our method—search for matching pairs with nothing separating them.

Can you work out who the undercover cop is?

What is their code name?

83. Hitting Home

A member of the public has contacted you because they moved into a new house a month ago and have already had a break-in.

You discover that they've posted a lot about their new property on social media, along with several photos.

You don't know how the criminals got in, but you suspect you can use the posts to find out.

Recent posts from SammiRose:

1. Pick up the keys to the house tomorrow!

2. Ugh, holdups with the house move while they replace a rusty garage door in the new place. Better safe than sorry I guess?

3. Finally got the keys! Garage door replaced! Now with snazzy electronic keypad! An impossible-to-forget code, unlike the keys!

4. Sammy is too fat for his new cat flap *facepalm*. Gotta lock it up so we don't accidentally make any more feline friends

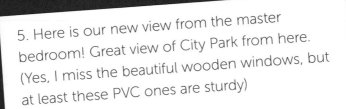

5. Here is our new view from the master bedroom! Great view of City Park from here. (Yes, I miss the beautiful wooden windows, but at least these PVC ones are sturdy)

6. Husband has managed to lose his keys and lock mine in the house so we will be entering our abode through the garage for the foreseeable! What a way to begin our home life—one week in!

7. Husband found his keys! They were in his pocket, obviously

8. Celebrating two weeks in the new place, and today is our fifth wedding anniversary—greatest day of our lives!

9. Three weeks we've been here and we still haven't taken the "SOLD' sign down—oops!

How do you think the criminals got in—and how did they know which house to go to?

84. Fight or Flight

The world of police work can be tedious, and more filled with paperwork than apprehending criminals. However, I count myself lucky to be a detective inspector whenever I speak to friends in the world of big business. The life of working fourteen-hour days before heading out to extravagant parties at expensive nightclubs simply does not appeal to me. I'd rather take the paperwork.

My aversion to this world was brought to the front of my mind not long ago while working on a case. My team was summoned to an almost impossibly high skyscraper in the financial district of London, where an advertising campaign manager, a woman named Helen MacLey, had been murdered. The crime appeared to have taken place around 10 p.m. the night before, when only a handful of people were left in the office, finishing off work. The murderer had been quite timely—Helen's assistant, who worked in the same office, had gone out to get some takeaway food from a nearby pizzeria, during which time the culprit had managed to slip into the office unseen and fire the fatal shot.

I put one of my officers in charge of securing the scene and asked another to take the understandably shaken assistant into a quiet room nearby and get her a cup of tea. I walked down the lengthy corridor to get the lay of the land, eventually coming to a room with a polished brass sign on the door: "Antonia Schumann, CEO'. The door was ajar, and when I pushed it open, I was stunned by the room's size—it felt like a tennis match would not be out of the question, if one moved the many expensively upholstered armchairs and glass coffee tables out of the way. It put my humble cubicle in New Scotland Yard to shame. I heard the door click behind me, and turned to see the CEO entering. "Sorry for keeping you waiting,' she said in only slightly flustered tones, "my flight in from JFK was delayed. I've just heard the awful news about Helen—is there anything I can help with?'

I asked her if she could elaborate on Helen's role in the company, and if she knew of anyone who held a grudge against her.

"She was a very forthright person; I think she rubbed people the wrong way sometimes. She was never afraid to say exactly what she thought. Martin, another campaign manager here, couldn't stand her, which often caused problems that I could have done without. They ended up at each other's throats in meetings, and I sometimes had to send them both out to cool off. Helen always had excellent ideas though and was very good at getting to the heart of what people wanted to get out of their campaigns. I've just gotten back from a meeting with a new client, actually; we spent a couple of days talking through a new project, and they've commissioned us. I was planning on giving the campaign to Helen to manage—she and the assistant had met the CEO a few years ago, and they had all gotten along well.'

This Martin character seemed interesting, and I tracked him down as soon as I could for an interview. He was a tall guy in his midthirties, with a disarming smile that almost succeeded in concealing the flinty ruthlessness in his eyes. I asked him about his relationship with Ms. MacLey, and where he had been at the time of the murder.

"I was on the other side of town at a work party, so no help to you there I'm afraid! Got there at nine-ish—hundreds of people can confirm it. I hadn't even seen Helen since that morning when she ignored me by the coffee machine. She could be incredibly rude sometimes. I've been chosen to manage several big campaigns recently, and I think she resented me for it. Hammering at the glass ceiling and all that. But whatever you say about equality in the workplace, I'm just better at thinking up ad campaigns, and I think senior management saw that. Mind you, she had a funny way of finding things out about people as well, and she'd drop the strangest things into conversation in a way that made people quite nervous sometimes. But anyway, that's not what you want to know—I'm not sure who could have done it really. That assistant has always been a funny one—quiet type, but that look in her eye that puts you a bit on edge. I know they went out together occasionally, but I got the sense Helen just wanted to keep her sweet so she didn't mind working late so much."

At this point, Martin called out to a tall gangly young man who happened to be passing. "Hey, Clinton, weren't you here working late last night?" Clinton seemed unimpressed at such an introduction to a police officer, but replied with quiet confidence.

"I was here, yes—I'm a designer, and sometimes the campaign managers come up with ideas that are so involved they keep me up all night." (At this point in his narrative a cold look was directed at Martin.) "My office isn't far from Helen's, and I did hear some voices in the corridor at around ten fifteen, but I didn't think anything of it."

I returned to the room where the assistant had been sitting, and found she had finished her tea and was ready to speak with me. I started by asking her what Ms. MacLey had been like both as a manager and as a person.

"She wasn't always the easiest person to work for—she'd worked hard to get to the top of her game, and she wasn't afraid to cut down anyone who stood in her way or threatened her career somehow. She was great fun if she was in a good mood—she took me out for lunch sometimes, and we'd always end up in fits of laughter. But I wouldn't want to get on her bad side. I remember a few weeks ago our CEO, Antonia, held a meeting about a new Italian client the company was producing a campaign for, and the whole thing descended into mayhem when Martin and Helen locked horns. Antonia wanted someone to go out and work with the client in Rome to get the ball rolling, and Helen was desperate to go—or maybe just to be chosen over Martin. Antonia would usually have gone herself I think, but she's just had a baby and is trying to cut down on traveling—I organize her schedule too, and she hasn't left England in a few weeks. In any case, the whole thing was very awkward—you should have heard the things they said to each other. Would probably have gotten you fired anywhere else but people seem to set store by 'passionate' creativity here. I wasn't sure what either of them wouldn't do to get one up on the other."

Lastly, I had a brief chat with the doorman of the building, a good-natured young man who claimed it was his first job. He said:

"I know the woman you mean. She always wore such bright colors—she was usually quite friendly, although you know how these city types can be sometimes. Wrapped up in their own affairs and no time to chat. Her assistant on the other hand, she's really nice—always stops to ask how I am. I saw her go out for pizza last night when it happened. She even gave me a slice on her way back."

I looked out of the tall windows at the front of the building to the street beyond and stood lost in thought for a moment while I watched the commuters start to trickle out of the tall buildings, maneuvering their rucksacks and briefcases through the busy streets, heading for home.

I felt sure that something that didn't quite add up, but I couldn't put my finger on what it was. However, as is often the way, it sprang back to me later while I was chopping vegetables for dinner.

What was it?

85. Undercover Officer

You're the advance member of a notorious criminal gang, and you're planning your most audacious hit yet: you aim to steal a world-famous trophy from right in front of a packed audience.

You figure that none of them will know the intended order of proceedings, so none of them will intervene to stop you from picking up the trophy and making off with it, while similarly no one could possibly suspect that anyone would plan to steal something from in front of thousands of spectators!

But your intuition is acting up. You caught a glimpse of something suspicious in this particular section of the crowd, shown to the right.

What is it that makes you think that one of these people is an undercover officer? Which person is it?

86. Clues from a Crook

Many of the criminals you have apprehended have been relatively unimaginative. However, recently you have been on the case of someone quite different.

She's a mathematician, and somehow she's managing to break into complex online banking systems which should be completely hackproof.

You and your partner have hired someone to hack into *her* computer, so that you can get ahead of her as she lines up her next target. The hacker manages to remotely gain access to her hard drive, but everything is strangely encrypted.

A message flashes, asking for a number key to access the information on her computer.

As he tries a few combinations, you and your partner both receive an email that seems to be from the mathematician:

```
        So you want to get into
           my database, huh?

      You only had to ask nicely!

     Here's the access code—kinda.

    I'm sure you can fill in the rest.

         Catch me if you can!
```

In an attachment, you see she's sent lots and lots of numbers! At first glance, you can't see how this is going to help you solve the code:

1	4	9	16	25	36	__
2	3	5	7	11	13	__
1	2	3	5	8	13	__
1	8	27	64	125	216	___

You look over at the hacker, who's at a loss.

Looking more closely, however, you realize she really has given you clues that will let you uncover the access code.

The screen shows the following message:

Access Code Required:

‐ ‐   ‐ ‐   ‐ ‐   ‐ ‐ ‐

What should you enter?

87. The Holdup

"On your knees! Now!'

You've just broken into a bank, and your team has the deputy manager and her colleagues held hostage.

To your annoyance, however, it turns out that the manager hasn't trusted any of them with the full details of the combination to the vault. Looks like they've been expecting some trouble.

Five employees all hold some of the details, and only when the information from all of the employees is combined can you find the correct combination.

You can see from the door that you need three digits, and your familiarity with this style of safe lock means that you are also sure that none of those digits will repeat—so you are looking for three different digits.

It takes several minutes to try any one combination, so you can't just keep guessing –and anyway, it would take too long.

You soon learn from the five employees that each knows a different three-digit number, of which only one digit is actually contained in the vault combination.

After some gentle persuasion, you get your hostages to reveal a little more about what they know.

You learn the following about each combination:

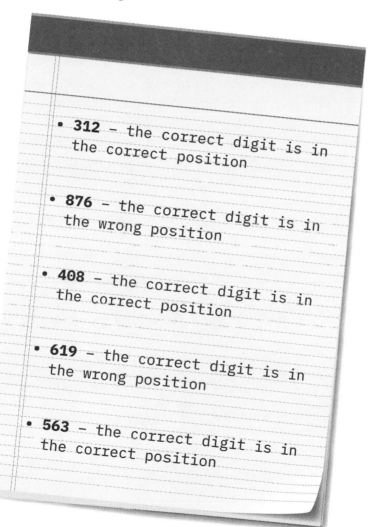

- **312** – the correct digit is in the correct position

- **876** – the correct digit is in the wrong position

- **408** – the correct digit is in the correct position

- **619** – the correct digit is in the wrong position

- **563** – the correct digit is in the correct position

What is the combination to the safe?

88. Time to Travel

Some criminals seem to always be one step ahead. As soon as you work out where they're hiding out and organize a raid, you find they've vanished without a trace.

You've been tracking down one such perpetrator recently, and you think following his every action is the key to predicting his next move—so you've been keeping a very close eye.

You took a day off yesterday and left it to the rest of your team to keep tabs on him.

Unfortunately, the notes you have gathered from other investigators on the case are far from clear.

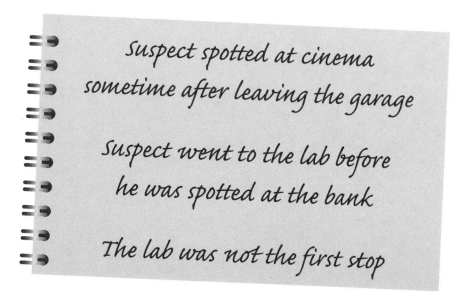

Suspect spotted at cinema sometime after leaving the garage

Suspect went to the lab before he was spotted at the bank

The lab was not the first stop

You know that he went to six different places
yesterday and visited each place exactly once.

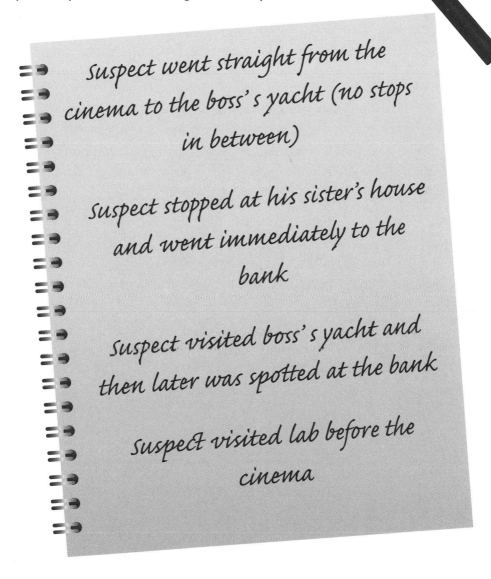

Suspect went straight from the
cinema to the boss's yacht (no stops
in between)

Suspect stopped at his sister's house
and went immediately to the
bank

Suspect visited boss's yacht and
then later was spotted at the bank

Suspect visited lab before the
cinema

Can you decipher the clues to unravel the order in which the criminal
visited each location?

89. Storeroom Break-in

You've just broken into an electronics shop, hoping to make off with some of the latest releases—but it seems that the store manager's security measures are more rigorous than usual, and no single employee knows the whole combination to the stockroom.

Each of four employees knows a single digit, and each has a scrap of paper in their wallet or purse that helps them remember what it is. You've collected these scraps, as shown below. Can you now work out the four-digit combination?

A: Never trust anyone—that's what I have learned over the years.

B: Robbers always target big technology stores when they get bored.

C: Count the letters—that's what I say. Customers love us. See?

D: Don't give in to their demands, they will never decipher this code. Don't be d-d-dumb.

90. Missing Microchip

"I'm a billionaire. A lot of people want a slice of this pie."

That's what my latest client told me as I opened an investigation into a recent incident in his home.

I'd woken up to a phone call in the middle of the night. Something urgent, I was told, something that needed my attention straightaway. Of course, anyone who's a victim of crime thinks that their case is the most important—but something about this situation got my attention immediately.

He wasn't lying—he's a billionaire indeed, whose name you've almost certainly heard. He has extremely widespread interests, and earned his money in computing; a tech giant, you might say. Since then, he's invested in a whole range of projects—some cryptocurrency, lots of charity work, property portfolios, transport, pharmaceuticals... He knows a lot of people, and has fingers in lots of pies. Let's call him Mr. Smith.

Being a tech giant, you'd think he'd have created a way to back up his most important information and keep it away from prying eyes. I'm no computer genius, but I figured it surely couldn't be that difficult to create a system that encrypted your private details and assets online, if you wanted to, so that nobody could access them—and especially if you appeared to own half of the internet. But that's neither here nor there.

The fact is, our billionaire had decided to save all of his most sensitive information on a microchip that he kept in his closely guarded home—a hard copy, if you like. It's quite an old-school way of doing things, but unfortunately for him the nostalgic technique hadn't paid off: the microchip had gone missing at some point during the previous day.

When I met him in the early hours (he sent a very nice car to collect me—after I laughed off the offer of a helicopter), it was obvious that the investigation was to be conducted in absolute secrecy. He was the only person who knew the chip had been stolen (except for whoever took it), and he wanted to keep it that way—presumably to give him the upper hand and lead the perpetrator into a false sense of security. One thing was made clear to me from the start: it was a matter of international importance that this microchip was returned to its rightful owner, and fast. This guy has friends in very high places and it wasn't hard to imagine the kind of information he might have on world leaders, political gatekeepers and even perhaps shadier characters whose names he wouldn't want to divulge.

The billionaire informed me that there was nothing on there that was *personally* incriminating—but that there was a lot of information that was very sensitive indeed. I decided to take him at face value and start looking for the missing item.

The chip had been stored in a secure secret room just off his study that also functioned as a panic room, presumably so that the billionaire could hide himself along with his precious technology if anyone untoward came knocking. He said he usually had people coming in and out of the house all day, but there were only two live-in staff: his secretary and his housekeeper.

First off, I asked the man himself what his movements had been yesterday. He said the morning was wide open—unusual for him—so he'd had a leisurely breakfast by the pool, and sat in the hot tub for a bit, although he had refrained from taking a swim. There was a prelunch meeting with his secretary in the kitchen, and they left the house just after 1 p.m. Lunch was with a mentee of sorts, then he and the secretary drove to a local school to open a science department, then came back here to drop off the car. Having firmed up his plans for the following day, he left for dinner with a friend from university at a local restaurant and returned just before midnight. Other than that, nothing worth noting.

Next, I spoke to the secretary, a man called Evan—although I realize I never found out if that was a surname or a first name. The billionaire had told me he had last seen the microchip at 1 p.m., and by midnight it had gone, so I asked Evan what he had been doing between those hours.

"Well, most of that time I was with the man himself: we left here around one o'clock to go for lunch with a local entrepreneur who Mr. Smith has been a kind of mentor to. We'd spent the previous few hours preparing for it, downstairs in the kitchen actually. We were going to take the helicopter to the meeting, but instead Smith wanted to drive—he had the valet bring his favorite car around, and we drove with the roof down. I often attend meetings with Mr. Smith—he's a generous man, and he involves me in his business decisions too. He calls me his right-hand man, although I'm not sure that's a title I'm worthy of.

"After lunch—it ended around half past three—I accompanied Mr. Smith to the opening of a school science department some distance away. He likes to show his face in the area; people always assume he'll be flanked by security, but he's a pretty humble guy and he likes to stay down to earth. We were there for an hour or so—took a tour around the school—and then we came back here and discussed the schedule for today. Actually, we are supposed to be heading up the coast this morning in just an hour or so to a new university building opening—funded by Mr. Smith, of course—but something's thrown him off; I always try to keep him to his schedule. But anyway, I'd say we got back here around six—the valet would be able to tell you for sure, as we dropped the car off with him.

"Mr. Smith wasn't here in the evening—he was out for dinner with an old friend. I ate dinner outside around eight o'clock—Rosie made me a delicious salad. It was warm outside, and I'd gotten a little sunburned with the top down in the car, so I relaxed for a bit in the hot tub and then went to bed. Mr. Smith lives alone—except for Rosie and me, of course—so he doesn't mind us using the facilities when he's out. In fact, even when he's in, he treats us as though this is our home too. He's a kind man, really; a simple one. Sometimes I think this fame and fortune is wasted on him—he has all that power, and that obscene bank account, and just lives a pretty ordinary life.

"I must have been in bed by about 10 p.m.—I said goodnight to Rosie just before I went upstairs—and watched an episode of an old show I like. I slept pretty poorly—the windows in my room are stuck shut, and the heat is unbelievable—and when I got up around dawn this morning, Smith was already pacing around his study looking like the workaholic he is. I'd better ask him if he's ready to leave for this university trip."

I thanked Evan for his time. It sounded like he'd had a pretty ordinary day, and it matched with what Mr. Smith had told me, so I let him go off and find his employer to discuss the next item on their agenda.

Next was the housekeeper, a woman named Rosie. I asked her what she was doing yesterday and whether anyone suspicious had come to the house.

"Well, it was a Wednesday so it was linens day. We have everything sent out to be washed, and new linens come in, fresh and ironed, and I put them on the beds. There are only eight bedrooms here, you know—people assume Mr. Smith must live in the lap of luxury with dozens of rooms and a private restaurant. Although I suppose he does have a pool. And a helipad.

"Anyway, Mr. Smith didn't want any lunch yesterday—he was out for a meeting, and Evan went with him. They left around one o'clock, although they'd spent most of the time leading up to it in the kitchen with me, having an informal meeting about it. The linens company arrived about 1:30 p.m., just after they left, and for the next few hours I was sorting that out, putting the sheets on the beds, making everything up just so. I do it all myself, and the linens people just came and went quickly, as usual. I'm a bit of a perfectionist, and I like a job to be done well.

"At about 4 p.m. a window technician came around to have a look at Evan's window—all this heat, and the poor man has his window stuck shut! He was here for about an hour, but he'll be back later today—he didn't have the right parts yesterday, so the thing still won't open. The valet appeared in the kitchen asking for an iced coffee—a sweet boy, with nothing much to do most of the time. That must have been while they were on their way back from the school tour. In fact, I think they got back around 6 p.m., as I remember him scuttling off to the front door to greet them. Ah, and a technician had been around to sort the hot tub out—something needed fixing. That was about 5 p.m.—though he's coming back any time now to fill it back up again, so you can ask him then about yesterday if you like.

"I made a salad for Evan, and he had that around eight o'clock on the veranda. Mr. Smith was dining out with an old friend, so I ate my salad indoors—by the fan—and cleaned up the kitchen. I was just finishing up when Evan came down to say good night; that must have been around 10 p.m. I locked up then, took a cool shower, and went to bed. I fell asleep rather quickly, but I heard Mr. Smith come back in at midnight, since the noise woke me up.

"Today I got up early to let the gardener in through the gates, and the window technician is coming back later too. It's a funny house, this one—buzzing all day long with people, valets and linens and personal trainers and guests—but in the evening, it all goes quiet. Mr. Smith isn't much of a party animal, which I'm grateful for, and you'd never think he hobnobs with the rich and famous during

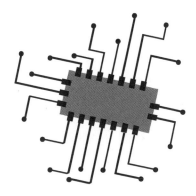

the day. But never mind about that—would you like an iced coffee?'

I politely declined her offer, but thanked her for the information she'd given me. She seemed like a trustworthy woman, and I was satisfied with her version of events.

By the sound of it, there were plenty more people I could have questioned, either as suspects or just to corroborate Rosie's story: the valet, the linen company, the pool technician, the window technician, and maybe more.

But I'd already caught somebody in a lie, and that was certainly going to be my next line of inquiry. Of the three stories I'd heard already, what particular contradiction stood out?

91. Ransacked at Dawn

A company office in the city was broken into in the early morning. The thief managed to get out within just a few minutes after the alarm was triggered, but they were hasty in their escape and left behind a trail of evidence.

How quickly can you take note of the many potential clues in this crime scene? Remember: anything out of place might later help you catch the culprit.

You have just one minute to scan the room. Then turn the page to see what you've remembered.

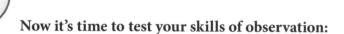

Now it's time to test your skills of observation:

1. What evidence is there that there was once a laptop or other electrical appliance on the desk?

2. What two finance-related elements were left behind at the scene?

3. How do you think the thieves made their escape?

4. What element of the scene would have required the knife to have been cut as shown?

5. There are various elements in the scene that might contain the thief's DNA, but there is one item in particular that—if it is the thief's—is the first item to test for this. What is it?

6. What has happened to the bin? Is there something on the desk that might have been removed from the bin and placed there?

7. Which element of the scene suggests that the thief was willing to get violent if they had had to do so?

8. What evidence left behind in the room might tell you something about the route that the thief took to this office?

92. Laser Focus

A priceless jewel is on display in a traveling exhibition, and of course you must have it at once. Can you negotiate the many laser traps within the exhibit to make it to the jewel without setting off an alarm?

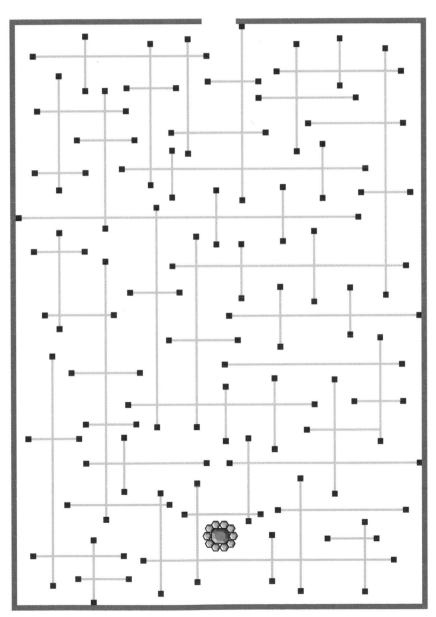

Solutions

1. Fast Frequency

The correct frequency is 26, which can only be formed from 7, 9, and 10. All the other totals can be made in multiple ways:

- 18 can be made by 3+7+8 or 8+10
- 22 can be made by 3+7+12, 3+9+10 or 10+12
- 30 can be made by 3+7+8+12, 3+8+9+10 or 8+10+12
- 34 can be made by 7+8+9+10 or 3+9+10+12

2. The Phone PIN

The PIN is 4567.

3. Liar, Liar?

Harriet is lying, and Holly is telling the truth.

Holly and Harriet are contradicting each other, so at least one of them must be lying. If Harriet's statement that neither of them are liars is true, then Holly would have to be telling the truth—which would be a contradiction, so Harriet cannot be telling the truth. Holly is therefore demonstrably telling the truth. This would also mean that Holly has nothing to do with the charges she's been brought in on.

Solutions

4. Make Like an Artist

The differences are as follows:

5. The Apartment Crime

The murderer lives in apartment number 916.

6. The Sign on the Safe

Each of the numbers on the sign corresponds in turn with the number of letters in the text on the sign. The final two words are *the* and *safe*, so the final two numbers are 3 and 4.

7. Caught by Clothing

The thief's clothing is in Bag E.

Guest 4 is the only person who mentions socks, so Bag D must be theirs. From this, we can work out that Guest 3 must have left Bag C,

Solutions

and Guest 2 left Bag A, as they are the only remaining bags containing the items they left behind. Of the last two bags, only one contains the belt lost by Guest 1—Bag B. That means the only bag left must contain the thief's clothing.

8. All Mapped Out

The "×" should be drawn on the church shown at the end of the route below, highlighted on a zoomed-in section of the map:

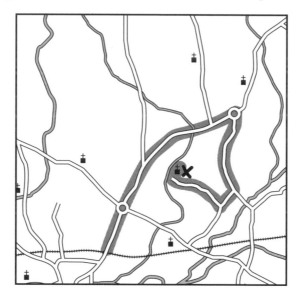

9. The Missing Diplomat

Basil's line manager mentions that the missing man rented an apartment from his sister-in-law (which could either be his spouse's sister or the wife of his sibling). At work, however, a colleague clearly states that Basil is an only child, and separately the government aide describes Basil as never having been married. Both of these seem to rule out the possibility of a sister-in-law existing, which in turn incriminates the man who made the claim: Basil's manager. Further,

Solutions

the manager exclusively uses the past tense to talk about Basil, which is in itself rather suspicious. Of course, this might be an affectation, and it could be that Basil himself has not been entirely honest with everyone when discussing his private life. But it's a potential lead.

10. The Artful Dodger

Your route is as follows:

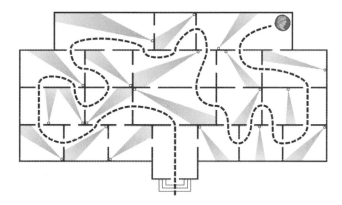

11. The Four Robbers

There were twenty-eight gold bars to start with, and the bars have been divided up as follows:

- A has sixteen bars
- B has eight bars
- C has four bars
- D has no bars

To work out how many bars there were to start with, start from the final break-in, where criminal D says there were no gold bars left for them to take. We know that C must have emptied the vault by taking half of what was there, plus two extra. For C to leave no bars, then "half

Solutions

of what was there" when they arrived had to be the same number as the extra two bars they were going to take with them, i.e. C takes half (two bars) and the two extra bars, meaning they've taken four bars in total and left nothing.

Now work back to when B arrives at the vault. To calculate what must have been in the safe, you must work backwards from the four bars you know are there when C arrives. The four bars are the result of B taking half plus two—so start by adding two to four, and then double it. That tells you there were twelve gold bars when B arrived—and they took half (six) plus two, meaning eight in total.

If we know there were twelve bars when B arrived, we can work out what A took, and therefore how many bars there were to start with. Add two to the twelve bars and then double it to get twenty-eight. There were twenty-eight bars to start with, and A took half (fourteen) plus two to make off with sixteen bars.

12. Blinded by the Light

The window lights create a braille message. This braille text reads ANTONIA—the name of the person you need to find.

13. Digital Disguise

The twelve-digit code is 153007051425. To find it, transform the times shown on the analog clocks into how they would appear on a digital twenty-four-hour clock: 15:30 for the first clock, 07:05 for the second, and 14:25 for the final one. Combine the three times to create the twelve-digit code.

Solutions

14. Find the Apartment

The correct apartment number is 989. Rather than using the mathematical operations as usual, they should be used to combine the segments of the numbers used in the digital-clockface font. To find the first number, start with 4 and add in all the segments of 3 in the same position, to result in 9. In other words, imagine overlaying one number on top of the other—and what new number would then result?

Overlaying the 5 and 2 results in an 8, and overlaying the 1 and the 5 results in a 9 (remembering that the 1 uses the two rightmost segments in the seven-segment number display).

15. The Eccentric Enigma

The safe code is 1257. Each line of compass points is a concealed instruction to draw a single digit, and the clue "travel using straight lines" indicates that you need to draw the digits using straight lines between the different compass points. For the first sequence, start at north and draw a straight line down to south to for the digit 1. Then carry on, spelling out one digit in each line, until you have the code 1257.

16. Home Sweet Home

The next three house numbers are 14, 1, and 11.

Your DS has worked out that, to create their social media name, each criminal shifted every letters of their real name along the alphabet by a certain number of letters—and that number matches their house number.

He has worked out that Marcus Leary lives at 15 Hannover Place, as the social media name Bpgrjh Atpgn is Marcus Leary shifted by fifteen places, and that Cathy Jaydon lives at 7 Green Lane (Jhaof Qhfkvu is shifted seven).

Solutions

Following this method, Jesse Winton lives at 14 Fairchild Avenue (Xsggs Kwbhcb is shifted fourteen), Larry Orsino lives at 1 High Street (Mbssz Pstjop is shifted one), and Helga Smith lives at 11 Dark Hill (Spwrl Dxtes is shifted eleven).

17. Mugged Off

The eyewitness was describing the person furthest to the right.

18. Gate-Crashing

The code to the gate is 746. Follow the instructions for each day to draw three separate paths on the map. Once the paths are complete, they reveal the three numbers, which can be read in the order of the days to reveal the code.

Here are the paths for each day from 1 to 3 in turn:

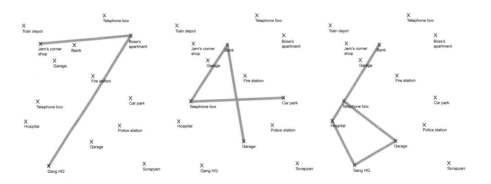

Solutions

19. Hack the Hacker

The values of each symbol are as follows:

= 7   = 5   = 3

The passcode is therefore 337357.

20. Multifaceted Problem

The number is 944568533. The correct order of the digits in the phone number is given by the numerical labeling on the shapes, while the number of sides on each shape gives the digit required. For example, 1 is on a nonagon, giving the first digit as 9.

21. Villainous Vacation

1. The first location is the Eiffel Tower, in France.

2. The second location is the Statue of Liberty, in the U.S.

3. The third location is Mount Fuji, in Japan. A part of the famous Chureito Pagoda is visible at the edge of the shot.

22. Old-School Cool

The next victim's initials are ALH. Ignoring their mouths, the eyes on the emoji symbols can be interpreted as Morse code, with one letter spelled out per message. The first emoji shows ··-, which is A. The second pair shows ·-··, or L, and the final pair shows ····, or H. So the victim's initials are ALH. The final message, "Gotta dash to be there on the dot!" is a hint that you'll need to use Morse code.

Solutions

23. Whispered Words

1. The criminals expressed an interest in diamonds
2. They were planning to use a Ford Mondeo as a getaway car
3. The robbery is supposed to take place on Bond Street
4. Two people were planning the robbery—a man and a woman
5. The consultation was booked for 3 p.m.
6. The corrupt banker is located in Mayfair

24. Missing Mole

The password is *Einstein* (or EINSTeIN). The hint suggests that you need to look at the periodic table of elements to find your solution. After the first letter E, the numbers in the clues refer to the atomic numbers of chemical elements, from which their lettered symbols spell out a solution:

- 53 = I (iodine)
- 7 = N (nitrogen)
- 16 = S (sulphur)
- 52 = Te (tellurium)
- 53 = I (iodine)
- 7 = N (nitrogen)

25. Pick Your Poison

Thallium was most likely the poison that was used. Presumably it was in the lasagna. The boss says it tasted normal, which rules out atropine with its bitter taste. Strychnine and cyanide can also be ruled out, as the boss survived for several days after ingestion. Hair loss suggests that the poison was either arsenic or thallium—and given the painful feet, thallium is the most likely candidate.

Solutions

26. Passcode Problem

The code you need is 847.

The completed sudoku looks like this:

4	3	8	2	7	5	1	6	9
7	9	1	3	6	4	2	5	8
2	6	5	9	1	8	3	7	4
8	2	6	5	9	1	7	4	3
1	5	3	8	4	7	9	2	6
9	4	7	6	3	2	5	8	1
6	7	4	1	5	3	8	9	2
5	1	2	4	8	9	6	3	7
3	8	9	7	2	6	4	1	5

The instruction "middle block, middle row, left to right, 3 digits" leads you to look at the three digits highlighted above—which gives you the code 847. This opens the door.

27. Dangerous Dialing

Your friend's phone number is 583 164 792. The solution to the sudoku is below, and this is the only horizontal nine-digit number that starts with a 5.

4	7	1	9	3	2	6	5	8
5	8	3	1	6	4	7	9	2
6	2	9	7	8	5	3	4	1
9	1	8	4	7	6	5	2	3
7	6	5	2	9	3	8	1	4
3	4	2	5	1	8	9	6	7
2	9	6	3	4	7	1	8	5
1	3	4	8	5	9	2	7	6
8	5	7	6	2	1	4	3	9

Solutions

28. Open the Vault

The access code is 628,762,814. The completed sudoku can be solved as below, and the diagonal that adds up to 44 is marked. You can work out which way to read it based on the 4 given at the end of the passcode entry prompt beneath the puzzle.

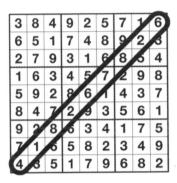

29. Double-Crossed?

The fail-safe code is 6482. The solved sudoku looks like this:

9	3	2	7	8	6	1	4	5
7	1	4	2	9	5	3	8	6
6	8	5	4	3	1	2	9	7
8	7	3	1	5	4	6	2	9
2	6	1	3	7	9	8	5	4
4	5	9	8	6	2	7	3	1
1	4	8	5	2	7	9	6	3
5	2	6	9	1	3	4	7	8
3	9	7	6	4	8	5	1	2

Your friend gave you a final clue of "even at the bottom" to find the four-digit code, which suggests you should take the even numbers from the bottom row. Reading from left to right, this gives you the code 6482. And now you're in!

Solutions

30. Taking Names

The next target will be the Guggenheim.

The "dates" next to each name tell you which letter to take from the first name and surname in each entry in the list. The date for the first entry is 01/02, so take the first letter of the first name and second letter of the surname, giving you G and U. Carry on in this way to spell the full location: GUGGENHEIM.

Unfortunately, this doesn't help you much—there are five Guggenheim museums all over the world, and you have no idea what they're planning or where. Looks like they'll get away with it this time...

31. Blooming Heck

The flower shown in the photograph (held up at the bottom left) is located here:

Solutions

32. The Drop

Leon is almost certainly lying.

Sara says that she looked through Leon's window at the start of her run, and the lights were off—but Leon and Jacques both state that Leon has blackout blinds, which were closed the night before, and which would presumably have stayed shut until 8 a.m. when Leon claims he woke up. If that's true, then Sara wouldn't have been able to look in and see all the lights off. So if Sara is telling the truth, and the blinds were up, then Leon is almost certainly lying about how long he was asleep for. Jacques was with Sara at the time, so we know she really did stop by Leon's.

Sara and Jacques both seem to have pretty strong alibis, made stronger by the fact that Jacques didn't even know that Sara would be able to verify his claim about gaming in the middle of the night; he didn't know it was her that he had messaged, or that she could see him online. It's possible that Sara and Jacques could both be lying and providing each other's alibis, but either way you have a lead. Now you and Martin will have to find some more missing pieces and work out who's the traitor.

33. A Clean Sweep

The murder weapon is the sculpture on the mantelpiece, which has a bloodstain on it. Along with this, there are a further seven splatters to find. It also looks like there was a hidden safe behind the painting, which presumably contained valuables—perhaps this is what the criminals were after.

Solutions

34. What a Wine-Up

There is a modern copyright symbol next to the name of the wine. This copyright symbol was not developed until the early twentieth century, although other ways of declaring copyright were used as early as the late seventeenth century.

35. Grid Glitch

The three-digit code is 506. To reveal each number, overlay the shaded squares of the boxes in each row to reveal the following:

36. Signaling Code

The date of your big break is May 31, 2022.

Throughout the message, Morse code has been hidden in the dots and dashes of the punctuation in each paragraph. Morse code is a "signaling code," as per the title—and this is also hinted at directly with *Morse* being the only capitalized word in the entire text.

You might also notice that each paragraph has five dots and dashes in total, which means that each of the eight paragraphs encodes a Morse number. The first paragraph, for example, contains three dots and two dashes when read in order, i.e. "· · · - -", which is the Morse code for the digit "3".

Looking at the punctuation paragraph by paragraph, the numbers are as follows:

Solutions

- · · - - -   = 3
- · - - - -   = 1
- - - - - -   = 0
- · · · · ·   = 5
- · · - - -   = 2
- - - - - -   = 0
- · · - - -   = 2
- · · - - -   = 2

This gives you the number string 31052022, i.e. 31/05/2022—which in European date format is 31 May 2022, or May 31, 2022.

37. Red Ruby Robbed

Solutions

38. The Drone

The missing area is 36 m².

Start by looking at the smallest room. It has an area of 12 m² and a width of 3 m, which means its missing length is 4 m. For the middle room, you're told it's a perfect square, so all four sides must be 5 m in length.

To measure the width of the largest room, take your known width of 5 m away from the 9 m given for the bottom side of the warehouse—which gives you a width of 4 m for the largest room. For the length of the largest room, add together the lengths of the two smaller rooms—4 m and 5 m—to give you 9 m².

The area of the largest room is therefore 4 m × 9 m, which is 36 m².

39. Caught Red-Handed

The prints connect like this:

Solutions

40. Getaway Car

The correct license plate is RT65 OCN (right-hand column, sixth down).

41. Cyber Scams

DaLLaS21 seems to be exaggerating. Although a lot of the various statements seem to agree with one another, not all of the timelines match up—and DaLLaS21's account seems to be the odd one out.

According to each candidate, these are their employment timelines:

DaLLaS21:
- Ten years ago—sets up HighLights and employs GamerGirl
- Seven years ago—GamerGirl leaves HighLights, and it is shut down by police
- Three years ago—ends career break and starts working with TOBI45

HintHint404:
- Four years ago—starts working for a gang
- One and a half years ago—leaves gang and takes a break
- One year ago—ends break and sets up cyber security firm with GamerGirl
- According to HintHint404, GamerGirl started working for HighLights six years ago—which was two years before HintHint404 started in the gang

GamerGirl:
- Six years ago—starts working at HighLights
- Three years ago—leaves HighLights, and it is shut down by police. Approached by TOBI45 and starts to work with him on Wormhole

Solutions

- Two years ago—leaves Wormhole when TOBI45 shuts it down, starts rival HighLights scheme
- One year ago—ends rival company and starts cybersecurity firm with HintHint404

TOBI45:
- Six years ago—sets up Wormhole
- Three years ago—employs GamerGirl for the last year of Wormhole
- Two years ago—shuts Wormhole down after four years
- Two years ago—starts working with HighLights founder
- According to TOBI45, he and DaLLaS21 began their previous schemes around the same time—so six years ago

As can be seen, DaLLaS21 seems to have added four years to the time he ran HighLights, and an extra year to his time with TOBI45. There are some serious gaps in his CV, and he doesn't seem to be the picture of honesty—so he probably shouldn't make the cut.

42. Money, Money, Money

The coin at the top of the right-hand page shows Hadrian wearing a crown—but on real Roman coin,s they did not wear crowns of this kind (at least not until hundreds of years after Hadrian), although they did sometimes wear laurels.

43. Cryptic Counsel

The money from the cryptocurrency is in an account that has $9m inside.

If the product of the amounts in the three accounts is $36m, and the

Solutions

accounts always have whole numbers in them, then you can work out the possible combinations of amounts that will give you $36m. You also know what the total amount across all three accounts adds up to a number that is the day of the month, which the person in the story will know. But how do you, as a reader, work the day out? The crucial point is that the person in the story does not know what the account totals are until they are sent a second email—the knowledge that there is one account with the "most" in is distinguishing between multiple options.

In fact, it turns out that only one potential day of the month has multiple options: the thirteenth. Of all the combinations of three factors that multiply to 36, only two combinations have numbers that add up to the same total: $1 \times 6 \times 6$, and $2 \times 2 \times 9$, where the sum of the numbers in both comes to 13. So today must be the thirteenth. From here, you can use the information that the illegal funds are in the account with the most money to choose the $9m account.

Now it's up to you to decide whether you trust your anonymous source...

44. Camera Clues

The correct passcode is the last one: 19 - 53 - 3 - 7 - 23. Of the five sets of numbers, it's the only one which does not come out to 100 when you add them all together:

- $42 + 19 + 23 + 7 + 9 = 100$
- $31 + 45 + 2 + 18 + 4 = 100$
- $62 + 4 + 17 + 10 + 7 = 100$
- $28 + 40 + 9 + 8 + 15 = 100$
- $19 + 53 + 3 + 7 + 23 = 105$

Solutions

45. Hidden in Plain Sight

1. Your surname is Batelli
2. The cartel boss is Harry Brown
3. Your mother is Scottish—so from Scotland
4. You were twenty-four when you went to prison
5. You'll be paid $2,500 at first—a third of the total fee
6. You first grew up in Liverpool

46. The Brothers Talk

Marco is the liar, Alessandro always tells the truth, and Mateo is the one who sometimes lies.

The first thing to notice is that Marco and Mateo both accuse Alessandro of being the occasional liar. This cannot be true, as if it were then it would create the impossible situation of one of the other two being a permanent liar but telling the truth about Alessandro's identity. Once Alessandro has been ruled out as the occasional liar, the other two can be ruled out as the honest brother, as they are both lying. So, Alessandro is the truth-teller. Once we know this, we can take his statement as truth—Mateo sometimes tells the truth (although he's lying at the moment), which leaves Marco as the one who lies all the time.

47. Road Less Traveled

The route you should follow to avoid the main roads is as follows:

Solutions

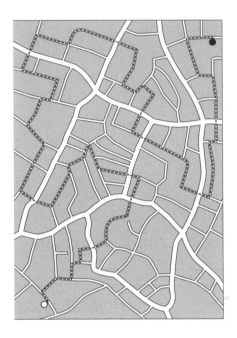

48. Friends on the Inside

- The escape will take place on Friday, between 3 and 4 p.m. We know it will be during visitation on Friday, as it's not during the weekend (ruling out Sunday's visitation) and not on a morning (ruling out Wednesday's visitation).

- The date of the escape will be Friday June 8. We know the week starts on Monday the fourth, so Friday would be the eighth.

- You will use the back gate: B told you not to use the side, and C told you not to use the front.

- B is driving the getaway car: A is not driving, and C has to stay inside after opening the gate remotely.

Solutions

49. Hidden Treasure

The diamonds are hidden in the sitting room of the house shown, which should be easy to identify now that you have the full floor plan. Once solved, the puzzle reveals the following floor plan:

This can be overlaid on the blank grid that contained room names on the opposite page. All of the rooms, bar one, have crosses (+), meaning they have nothing hidden in them. The only room that has a diamond-like picture is the sitting room—so this must be where the jewels are hidden.

50. Snake in the Graph

The passcode is 272 159 726 749 194. When complete, the path of the snake is as shown:

Solutions

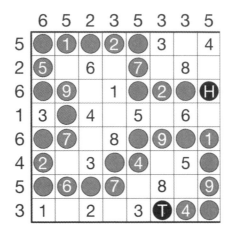

The path runs through the numbers 2, 7, 2, and so on when read from head (H) to tail (T), to create the full passcode.

51. Animal Instincts

Start by loading the lemur into the car and taking it to your HQ—seeing as you can't leave it alone with either the lynx or the food, it's got to come with you. Leave it there, and go back for the bag of food. Take the food to HQ, and then put the lemur *back* in the car—it can't be trusted alone with the food at HQ. Go back to the sanctuary, and swap the lemur for the lynx. Drop the lynx off at HQ (which won't want the lemur food); then finally go back to collect the lemur, bringing it back to HQ to complete the mission. You could also have reversed the order in which you took the lynx and the food—but the lemur has to come and go as described!

52. Password-Protected

The password is PORTAL. The instructions are directions to move around a standard QWERTY keyboard (see code book at the end of the book). Start at P on the keyboard and "push" to type a P. Then move

Solutions

one key to the left (to O) and "push", then five to the left (to R), and so on.

53. Valuable Pictures

The ten stolen items are circled:

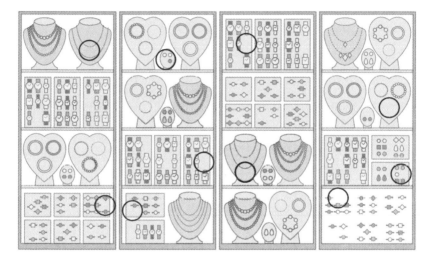

54. Membership Costs

It seems like Anders is lying. Firstly, he says he dropped off his car at the garage on Saturday afternoon and picked it up on Sunday morning—but Flinn says that Anders gave him a lift home in the scratched car on Saturday night, which would be impossible if it were at the garage overnight. Equally, Mel says she and Sammy saw Anders and his friend in the scratched car after midnight, which backs up Flinn's story—so Anders has not been honest about where his car was supposed to be nor when, or the fact that he claimed to be home by midnight.

There is an additional clue that doesn't seem to match up with what

Solutions

the others say: Sammy and Flinn saw each other in the park, and both clearly imply that the weather was good—between them, they're wearing shorts, a Hawaiian shirt, and sunglasses. They also make several references to the good weather—which agrees with what Mel says, who mentions getting a tan in the garden outside. Anders, on the other hand, mentions that he left the park around midday when the rain started—and then hung his laundry out to dry in the afternoon, which doesn't add up.

Equally, according to their stories, Anders, Sammy, and Flinn should all have been in the supposedly small park at the same time—but only Sammy and Flinn saw each other. It seems like Anders might not have been in the park at all and has made up a bogus reason for "leaving" it—as the weather was obviously good

Of course, Anders could have gotten the weather mixed up with the day before's, but there are a few things in his weekend that don't line up. It looks like Anders hasn't gotten his stories straight—and is trying to cross the wrong boss!

55. Home Visits

- The place with the pool belongs to the sports star, and they live in a detached house in Marylebone. Based on her final message, this is the house she'll be targeting.

- The place with the rooftop bar belongs to the singer—they live in an apartment in Mayfair.

- The place with the tennis court belongs to the actor—they live in a terraced house in Maida Vale.

Solutions

56. Notable Deception

The fake bank note is the one that has two *different* serial numbers on the same note, as shown by the dashed line:

57. The Great Escape

You'll be able to escape in forty-two hours. In that time (and including the final shift change), the guards working two-hour shifts will swap twenty-one times, the guards working three-hour shifts will swap fourteen times, and the guards working three-and-a-half-hour shifts will swap twelve times. In total, that's forty-seven shift swaps.

58. Go Phish

- "CJ" is a retired postal worker and will be telephoned about cryptocurrency

- "MP" is a software engineer and will be sent snail mail about their health insurance

Solutions

- "ZN" works for the government and will be emailed about their bank account

59. Wormholes

No. The worm will reach Device 5 in seventy-five minutes, i.e. after five fifteen-minute blocks.

- In the first fifteen-minute block, the worm will destroy 1TB on Device 1.

- In the second fifteen-minute block, the worm eats another 1TB (matching the previous session), plus the 2TB extra, for a total of 3TB. So after half an hour, it's eaten up 4TB in total: which is all the storage from Device 1.

- In the third fifteen-minute block, the worm eats 3TB (matching the previous session), plus the 2TB extra, which is 5TB. So after forty-five minutes, it's eaten all of Device 1's storage, and 5TB of Device 2's memory: 9TB in total.

- In the fourth fifteen-minute block, the worm eats 5TB (matching the previous session), plus the 2TB extra, which is 7TB. So after an hour, it's eaten all of Device 1's storage (4TB), all of Device 2's storage (5.5TB), and 6.5TB of Device 3's storage: 16TB in total

- In the fifth fifteen-minute block, the worm eats 7TB (matching the previous session), plus the 2TB extra, which is 9TB. So after an hour and fifteen minutes, it's eaten all of Device 1's storage (4TB), all of Device 2's storage (5.5TB), all of Device 3's storage (8TB), and all of Device 4's storage (7.5TB): 25TB in total.

- At the end of the seventy-five minutes, it will reach Device 5— where your financial information is stored—so you're going to be too late to stop it.

Solutions

60. Catch the Virus

The coordinates for the suspected cybercriminal are the first item on the list: 34°44'32.8"N 149°19'24.3"W

- 22°28'26.8"N 48°28'24.6"W contains only even digits
- 4°09'16.8"S 178°01'47.1"W is in the southern hemisphere
- 41°40'48.0"S 12°08'24.8"W is in the southern hemisphere
- 81°50'58.1"N 138°52'03.5"W is the most northerly location
- 55°15'53.9"N 31°17'37.5"W contains only odd digits

61. Identity Parade

The criminal is the first person on the second row. Numbering the people in the order 1 2 3 4 (top row), 5 6 7 8 (middle row) and 9 10 11 12 (bottom row), they can be eliminated as follows:

1. Eliminates 2, 4, 6, and 12
2. Eliminates 10
3. Eliminates 8 and 9
4. Eliminates 3
5. Eliminates 7
6. Eliminates 1 and 11
7. Leaves 5 as the criminal

Solutions

62. Burn After Solving

The airport you're flying to is JFK, in New York City. When solved, the grid looks like this:

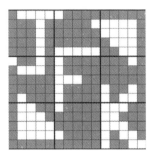

63. Don't Feed the Trolls

- rude_hanna's real name is Anna Hermosa—she posts on Instagram and lives in Buenos Aires

- 80schild's real name is Sam Bennet—he posts on Twitter and lives in New York City

- Tiny247's real name is Luc Dune—he posts on Facebook and lives in London

64. Stroke of Genius

907154. The punctuation in the text messages corresponds to numbers on a standard UK or US QWERTY keyboard (the differences between the two are not relevant to this puzzle). First, note that the first text says it is providing "key boarding information"—or "keyboarding information". Then the third text tells you to pay attention to punctuation. And the fifth text tells you to unshift yourself. So what you need to do is find the punctuation used in the texts on a keyboard, and "unshift" it back to the numbers that share the same keys. For

Solutions

example, the & in the second text "unshifts" to the digit 7, since pressing SHIFT and 7 would generate a & symbol.

There are six items of punctuation in the message, matching the six digits required, which can be decoded in order as follows:

- (= 9
-) = 0
- & = 7
- ! = 1
- % = 5
- $ = 4

This gives the code 907154.

65. Tattoo Terror

The matching symbol is the bottom-left one of the set, the three small spirals. It can be found right in the center of the torso, on the mouth of the skull.

66. Track the Tracks

The access code is 34 512 727 258. When solved, the tracks follow the path below:

Solutions

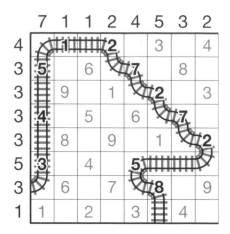

67. Message in a Bottle

The first line on each of the labels is an anagram of a day of the week from Monday to Friday. If you were to place the bottles side by side in a row, arranged in order by weekday, then you would be able to read a three-line message: "THE PEOPLE YOU SEEK ARE HIDDEN IN ROOM NUMBER TWENTY SEVEN HOTEL PARADISE NEW STREET".

68. A Date for Your Diary

Take the note left at the crime scene literally—it says to disregard everything in "THIS CLUE", so remove all of the letters found in these two words from the string of letters below. This leaves the message, "BARN BAR DOORMAN"—the person you should ask for more information, and their place of work.

69. The Newcomer

The texts are encoded as they would be typed on an old phone with a multitap typing system, where multiple presses of a number cycled

Solutions

through the various letters on each key. The number of times each number appears tells you how many times you would need to press that key in order to type the desired letter, so for example 2 = A, 22 = B and 222 = C. See the code book at the end of the book for a picture of a phone keypad.

Following this system, the decoded text messages read as follows:

GANG INFILTRATED

PLAN IS GO

MEET ME AT SIX PM

70. Rubbish Job

There is a pistol hidden as shown:

Solutions

71. All Blocked Up

The route is as follows:

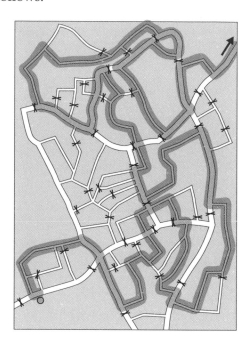

72. Crack the Code

The code is 66852. According to the subject line of the email, you need to "count capital totals"—which refers to capital letters in this case, not capital totals in a financial sense. The number of capital letters in each paragraph corresponds to the digit that that paragraph encodes:

the first thing to remember is that <u>ALL</u> money we make must be sent to our trusted <u>L</u>aundering <u>P</u>artners before it can be logged as "<u>I</u>ncome". (6)

wages are frequently reviewed. do <u>NOT</u> expect that you will earn the same as others. build trust over time, and <u>W</u>ork <u>Y</u>our <u>W</u>ay up. (6)

Solutions

our <u>H</u>Q (located in <u>L</u>ondon) holds all our <u>A</u>dministrative <u>R</u>ecords, so the location must be kept secret at <u>ALL</u> costs (8)

all income earned through <u>F</u>raud, <u>R</u>obbery, <u>B</u>lackmail, <u>A</u>bduction, <u>V</u>iolence, etc must be declared immediately—anyone found in possession of undeclared assets will suffer "punishment" (5)

we are not the only crew in the area so all cash, jewels, and other valuables must be stored in our safe. <u>T</u>he code is now in your possession, so you just have to find it… <u>R</u>ead each paragraph of this email carefully since there's one digit hidden in each—the subject line tells you how (2)

73. Got Your Number

Aitana Clemensen is implicated. The alphabet written at the bottom of the note gives you a clue—the note is written using a letter-number cipher, where each letter of the alphabet is substituted with a number: A=1, B=2, C=3 and so on, until Y=25 and Z=26. The deciphered note therefore reads as follows:

LOOK FOR THE PERSON WITH THE INITIALS AC

74. Binary Bust

The concealed message is as follows:

1745H
GARE DU NORD
PARIS

The "binary" numbers are indicators of which characters to keep and which to discard from the jumbled character strings. A 0 indicates to discard the corresponding character in that position

Solutions

in the corresponding string, while a 1 tells you to keep it. So, in the first character string A1T7M4G5WRH accompanied by the number 01010101001, the text "1745H" is revealed.

75. Internet Infiltrator

40424713007911. This is broken down as indicated by the corresponding square brackets, as follows:

- 404—"not found" code for an internet browser, as in "404 Not Found"
- 24/7—twenty-four hours a day, seven days a week
- 13—a baker's dozen
- 007—MI6 code number of James Bond
- 911—U.S. emergency phone number

76. Note to Self

The code is 917284. The numbers are concealed between certain pairs of words—for example, SEVEN is revealed in the pair APPLAUSE and VENGEANCE. The column on the right tells you how many letters of the relevant number are in the first and second columns respectively. Given that you know the first and last columns are in the correct order, you can work out how much is missing from each number given the information you have. For example, the first line has MARTINI in the first column and (2, 2) in the final column—so you need to take the last two letters of MARTINI—NI—and match them with the two letters at the start of a word in the second column to create a number. In this case, MARTINI can be matched with NEWSPAPER to make NINE.

Match up all pairs of words that reveal a number in this way, and read down the list to show the full password:

Solutions

MART<u>INI</u>	<u>N</u>EWSPAPER	= NINE
COLLUS<u>ION</u>	<u>E</u>NGINE	= ONE
APPLAU<u>SE</u>	<u>V</u>ENGEANCE	= SEVEN
HINDSIGH<u>T</u>	<u>W</u>ORKSHOP	= TWO
SL<u>EIGH</u>	<u>T</u>HUNDER	= EIGHT
WOL<u>F</u>	<u>OUR</u>SELVES	= FOUR

77. Phone a Friend

As hinted at in the subject line of the email, you are looking for "first things": the first letters of every word taken together in order spell out a series of numbers, giving the phone number 7249431524:

Seems even virtual extorters need (SEVEN) to watch out (TWO). For our undercover representatives (FOUR), new information naturally emerges (NINE)—ferret out uninformed reps (FOUR), they have restricted efficiency. Evaluate (THREE) our notable emissaries (ONE)—find informants. Vet everyone (FIVE) thoroughly: watch, observe (TWO). Fraudulent operations undo resolutions (FOUR).

78. High-End Burglary

The item that is likely to cause the least suspicion if you're searched, but represents the highest likely value, is the car keys—which could be yours, but are for the car that they will unlock and let you drive away. Hopefully.

For the other objects, while there are some items that may be valuable, such as the painting and vase, even if they *are* valuable, they are probably highly identifiable (and thus difficult to dispose of), and so it

Solutions

is best to pick the more general items. The trophy may be valuable, but it is hard to judge from the picture, and it may also be identifiable if a personalized award.

The remaining most valuable items are therefore likely to be as follows:

79. Unreliable Witness

The clock shows a time of just before 3:45, which doesn't correspond with the witness statement saying that they heard the window smash in the evening and then saw the burglar flee.

80. A Risky Experiment

You should arrest someone called Ana de la Selva. The four "chemical substances" are actually coordinates to be read from the chart. The first line, for example, tells you to look in cells C4, A2 and D3—which have A, N, and A in them, respectively.

Solutions

When all of the coordinates from each line are read from the chart, they spell out the name ANA DE LA SELVA.

81. What the Spies Say

This hidden message is DO NOT DUPE SPIES. Each sentence conceals a word used in the standard phonetic alphabet used by NATO—some of the words are split across multiple words in a sentence. Each paragraph conceals one word of the four-word message. The NATO code words are underlined below:

Our business mo<u>del ta</u>kes some time to understand fully—we don't just hire anyone, however good their credentials, so we have decided to send you on a simple mission to see what you can do. You have a reputation as an agent wh<u>o's car</u>eful, enterprising, and sympathetic to our cause—but keep in mind that we are watching, and this is your chance to spell it out to us.

We have been laying the groundwork for this mission since last <u>November</u>, so all you should need to do is carry out the final steps and pick up the documents. The documents we need are hidden in a filing cabinet in the NATO building, and you will gain access to it as a special delivery worker wh<u>o's car</u>rying a package for a member of senior management. Everything is organized, and the plan should work, but be careful—NATO has eyes and ears everywhere, and if they get a heads-up that they are playing host to a charla<u>tan, Go</u>d help you.

The building itself is something of a fortress—once you have used your fake documentation to breach the walls of this cita<u>del, ta</u>ke special care to examine your surroundings so you can find your way out. Your <u>uniform</u> (which we will send to you soon) should mean that few will question you, but getting lost could jeopardize your cover story, as the delivery person you are impersonating knows the building like

Solutions

the back of his hand. When you get to the filing cabinet containing the documents, work quickly, but pay attention, and do not mess it up—apart from anything else, any mistakes here will mean the end of our association. Remember, we chose you for your skills in exactly this area, but you have to prove yourself capable.

Once we have made it clear that we are in possession of the main dossier, ramifications for NATO will reveal themselves, and they will be severe. If you pull this off, it will be quite a feather in your cap—a payoff for your hard work so far. In terms of next steps, we are sending you a package that will contain diagrams of the building—make sure to study these in detail. As you will discover, once you are inside, you will have three choices of routes to get to the filing cabinet. I'll sign off for now—we will organize a meeting before long, and it will be easier raising any questions in person.

82. Double Agent

The name of the undercover cop is Greta Stone. Each sentence in the body of the letter has one word featuring a double letter, as hinted at by the title "Double Agent" and the text in the letter's postscript. Extract these letters from each sentence to spell out the first and last names— one per paragraph.

The double letters are highlighted below:

I am so glad you suggested infiltrating this group, since it is going to be quite a coup for our team when we take their leader into custody. In fact, I think the interrogation might end up being the highlight of my working life. But you need to be careful—they won't trust you straightaway. Take your time settling into the gang, and make sure they think of you as one of their people before you take any action. Aaron is going to be your main point of contact here, since you have worked together many times, and I trust him with the task.

Solutions

As for your undercover name, only those who absolutely must know should have it—it becomes a tricky business otherwise. We must avoid you getting into trouble. Good thing we have a system already for hiding such things—just search for the name in the usual way. Try to get into the inner circle of the group if you can, since it should be easier to find things out if you are trusted. Everyone here agrees that you are the best chance we have.

83. Hitting Home

You suspect that the criminals entered the house through the garage door, which evidently provides access to the house too, based on the posts.

Given that the garage door is no longer rusty and the windows are secure, you can assume it wasn't a physical weakness here that allowed them to break in—and if the cat flap is too small for a cat, it's unlikely that a person is able to squeeze through and break in. Instead they used the couple's wedding anniversary date as the code for the electronic keypad—a good guess, since the code is something "impossible to forget". The criminals could figure out the date of the anniversary from the relevant social media post.

Given the person posted the view from their master bedroom, it was evidently possible to identify the general location of their house, especially as they have said they live within view of a specific park. Finally, they didn't take the "SOLD" sign down for several weeks, so having narrowed it down sufficiently, it would have been relatively easy to establish which house was the one that was recently moved into—and had an electronic garage keypad.

Solutions

84. Fight or Flight

The assistant claims that Antonia's schedule (which she manages) has contained no travel out of England for weeks, but when Antonia appears at the offices, she claims that her flight from JFK has delayed her.

Given that JFK airport is in New York City, and the office building is described as being in London, this would certainly be considered traveling outside of England. So either the assistant is lying, or Antonia is. It shouldn't be too difficult to prove whether Antonia took the flight or not. But on top of that, the assistant seems to have a pretty solid alibi, so keep a close eye on Antonia while you carry out your next search.

85. Undercover Officer

The person two from the right-hand end of the middle row is wearing a wired earpiece in a single ear, with a curved wire rather than a standard headphone wire. Perhaps it's nothing, but you can't be too careful! Better not go ahead with the plan after all.

86. Clues from a Crook

The code is: 49 17 21 343. Each of the lines of numbers is a well-known mathematical sequence, with a missing number at the end:

- The first sequence is square numbers: 1, 4, 9, 16, 25, 36. The next number is 49.

- The second sequence is prime numbers: 2, 3, 5, 7, 11, 13. The next number is 17.

Solutions

- In the third sequence, each number is the sum of the previous two: 1, 2, 3, 5, 8, 13. So the next number is 21.

- The final sequence is cubed numbers: 1, 8, 27, 64, 125, 216. The next number is 343.

87. The Holdup

The correct combination is 462.

88. Time to Travel

The criminal visited the locations in the following order:

1. Garage
2. Laboratory
3. Cinema
4. Boss's yacht
5. Sister's house
6. Bank

89. Storeroom Break-in

The code is 6429. As clue C hints, you need to count the letters in each note that are listed at the start of that clue—so count the number of A's in the first clue, the number of B's in the second clue and so on. (If you try including the letter prompt itself, you'll go past nine on the final note, resulting in too many digits).

- **A:** Never trust anyone—that's what I have learned over the years. **6 a's.**

- **B:** Robbers always target big technology stores when they get bored. **4 b's.**

Solutions

- C: <u>C</u>ount the letters—that's what I say. <u>C</u>ustomers love us. See? **2 c's.**

- D: <u>D</u>on't give in to their <u>demand</u>s, they will never <u>d</u>ecipher this co<u>d</u>e. <u>D</u>on't be <u>d</u>-<u>d</u>-<u>d</u>umb. **9 d's.**

90. Missing Microchip

Evan says he relaxed in the hot tub in the evening, but Rosie says that a technician will be coming around later to "fill it back up again"—implying there was no water in it the night before. Of course either one of them might be the liar, but it would only take a minute to walk outside and see whether the hot tub was empty or not. If it was, Evan hasn't been entirely truthful about his activities—and if he wasn't in the hot tub, then what *was* he doing at that time?

91. Ransacked at Dawn

1. There is an electrical cable running to the desk.
2. A credit card on the desk and a banknote on the floor.
3. Through the open window, which they might have unlocked with the key on the desk.
4. The severed wire on the floor.
5. The glove is most likely the thief's and left behind by accident in their panic to leave. If they wore it, it will contain their DNA.
6. It has been knocked over—some torn paper, perhaps from the bin, is on the desk.
7. They brought a knife with them.
8. There is a muddy or dusty footprint on the floor—so the thief must have recently passed through such an environment.

Solutions

92. Laser Focus

The route is as follows:

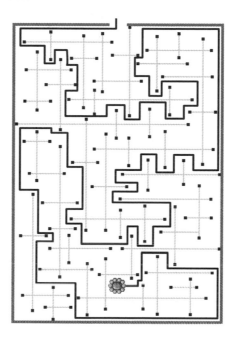

NATO Radio Code Words

A – Alfa	N – November
B – Bravo	O – Oscar
C – Charlie	P – Papa
D – Delta	Q – Quebec
E – Echo	R – Romeo
F – Foxtrot	S – Sierra
G – Golf	T – Tango
H – Hotel	U – Uniform
I – India	V – Victor
J – Juliett	W – Whiskey
K – Kilo	X – X-ray
L – Lima	Y – Yankee
M – Mike	Z – Zulu

Morse Code

A ·—	M ——	Y —·——
B —···	N —·	Z ——··
C —·—·	O ———	1 ·————
D —··	P ·——·	2 ··———
E ·	Q ——·—	3 ···——
F ··—·	R ·—·	4 ····—
G ——·	S ···	5 ·····
H ····	T —	6 —····
I ··	U ··—	7 ——···
J ·———	V ···—	8 ———··
K —·—	W ·——	9 ————·
L ·—··	X —··—	0 —————

Braille

A B C D E F G H I J

K L M N O P Q R S T

U V W X Y Z

The Periodic Table

1 **H** Hydrogen								
3 **Li** Litium	**4** **Be** Beryllium							
11 **Na** Sodium	**12** **Mg** Magnesium							
19 **K** Potassium	**20** **Ca** Calcium	**21** **Sc** Scandium	**22** **Ti** Titanium	**23** **V** Vanadium	**24** **Cr** Chromium	**25** **Mn** Manganese	**26** **Fe** Iron	**27** **Co** Cobalt
37 **Rb** Rubidium	**38** **Sr** Strontium	**39** **Y** Yttrium	**40** **Zr** Zirconium	**41** **Nb** Niobium	**42** **Mo** Molybdenum	**43** **Tc** Technetium	**44** **Ru** Rutenium	**45** **Rh** Rhodium
55 **Cs** Caesium	**56** **Ba** Barium	**57** **La** Lanthanum	**72** **Hf** Hafnium	**73** **Ta** Tantalum	**74** **W** Tungsten	**75** **Re** Rhenium	**76** **Os** Osmium	**77** **Ir** Iridium
87 **Fr** Francium	**88** **Ra** Radium	**89** **Ac** Actinium	**104** **Rf** Rutherfordium	**105** **Db** Dubnium	**106** **Sg** Seaborgium	**107** **Bh** Bohrium	**108** **Hs** Hassium	**109** **Mt** Meitnerium

58 **Ce** Cerium	**59** **Pr** Praseodymium	**60** **Nd** Neodymium	**61** **Pm** Promethium	**62** **Sm** Samarium	**63** **Eu** Europium
90 **Th** Thorium	**91** **Pa** Protactinium	**92** **U** Uranium	**93** **Np** Neptunium	**94** **Pu** Plutonium	**95** **Am** Americium

						2 **He** Helium
5 **B** Boron	6 **C** Carbon	7 **N** Nitrogen	8 **O** Oxygen	9 **F** Fluorine	10 **Ne** Neon
13 **Al** Aluminium	14 **Si** Silicon	15 **P** Phosphorous	16 **S** Sulfur	17 **Cl** Chlorine	18 **Ar** Argon

28 **Ni** Nickel	29 **Cu** Copper	30 **Zn** Zinc	31 **Ga** Gallium	32 **Ge** Germanium	33 **As** Arsenic	34 **Se** Selenium	35 **Br** Bromine	36 **Kr** Krypton
46 **Pd** Palladium	47 **Ag** Silver	48 **Cd** Cadmium	49 **In** Indium	50 **Sn** Tin	51 **Sb** Antimony	52 **Te** Tellurium	53 **I** Iodine	54 **Xe** Xenon
78 **Pt** Platinum	79 **Au** Gold	80 **Hg** Mercury	81 **Tl** Thallium	82 **Pb** Lead	83 **Bi** Bismuth	84 **Po** Polonium	85 **At** Astatine	86 **Rn** Radon
110 **Ds** Darmstadtium	111 **Rg** Roentgenium	112 **UUb** Ununbium	113 **UUt** Ununtrium	114 **UUq** Ununquadium	115 **UUp** Ununpentium	116 **UUh** Ununhexium	117 **UUs** Ununseptium	118 **UUo** Ununoctium

64 **Gd** Gadolinium	65 **Tb** Terbium	66 **Dy** Dysprosium	67 **Ho** Holmium	68 **Er** Erbium	69 **Tm** Thulium	70 **Yb** Ytterbium	71 **Lu** Lutetium
96 **Cm** Curium	97 **Bk** Berkelium	98 **Cf** Californium	99 **Es** Einsteinium	100 **Fm** Fermium	101 **Md** Mendelevium	102 **No** Nobelium	103 **Lr** Lawrencium

Codes 6/8

QWERTY keyboard

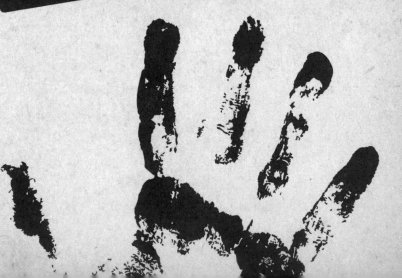

Phone Pad

Credits

Thanks to Becca Wright and Nicki Crossley for many of the criminal and detective situations, and to David Woodroffe for the illustrated puzzles.

Thanks also to Elizabeth Crowdy and Laura Jayne Ayres for their help in creating this book.

Dr. Gareth Moore

Additional images:
- p9, p160, p161 (notepad) Gstudio/Adobe Stock
- p29 (compass) Good Studio/Adobe Stock
- p43 (molecule) Visual Generation/Adobe Stock
- p56 (leaves on puzzle title) Gstudio/Adobe Stock
- p66 (speech bubble) Gstudio/Adobe Stock
- p216, p218, p220, p222 (paper background) Claudio Divizia/Adobe Stock
- p217, p219, p221 (dripping blood) vectortwins/Adobe Stock
- p219 (Braille) paul/Adobe Stock
- p222 (hand) lauritta/Adobe Stock
- All remaining nonpuzzle illustrations from pixabay